I0419941

"One cannot and must not try to erase the past merely because it does not fit the present."

Golda Meir

ৱ৹

Unraveling the Washington Web

KIM

JOHNSON

**why
networkingthe**
publishing

Unraveling the Washington Web

© 2016 by Kim Johnson

Editing by Kathie Wellman

Cover by Anne Ney

All Rights Reserved in all media. No part of this book may be used or reproduced without written permission, except in the case of quotations embodied in critical articles and reviews inclusive of research and educational articles.

The moral right of Kim Johnson as the author of this work has been asserted by her in accordance with the Copyright, Designs, and Patents Act of 1988.

All quotes used in this book fall under the Free Use Doctrine as they are being used to underscore and support my research, comments and criticisms. All quotes are cited under Notes for your personal access and review.

Published in the United States 2018 by

NetworkingTheWhy Publishing.

Print ISBN-13: 978-1539593782

ISBN-10: 1539593789

First Edition, 2016

Second Edition, 2018

For more information and to become part of
Networking the Why

Email me at: networkingthewhy@gmail.com
Or sign up for my blog www.kimhjohnson.com
to receive the latest commentary on current events
and this, that, and the other!

CONTENTS

ℰᴐ

NOTE TO READERS

ℰↄ

T his publication contains the opinions and ideas of the author. I've done my best to support all research, comments and criticisms with quotes from articles, journals, book and various websites. This book is intended to provide answers to the plethora of questions surrounding the 2016 election, the campaign and subsequent issues facing the Trump Administration. The author attempts to help the American citizen and all who watched 2016 election cycle in utter disbelief to understand "what was going on," "what is going on" and "what now?" In other words, why Trump?

The issues discussed are controversial and often connected to influential individuals within the Washington corridor. It is not the author's intent to disparage these individuals but to present the facts surrounding their connections within what I call, *The Washington Web*. This is not an "anti-anyone or anti-party" book. The author harbors no animosity or hatred towards the persons or organizations herein mentioned.

It is also not the intent of the author to incite hatred or any other attitude that would prove to be disrespectful or anti-American. The insights and expressions made throughout these pages are not necessarily the views of the contributing authors, individuals or organizations mentioned or cited within this book. The content is original to the author.

This book is dedicated to my mother, Georgia Johnson. She wrote the script for life and love on my heart through her continual example of courage, strength and sheer determination.

My mother taught me social responsibility from a very young age. Our home was a revolving door for neighbors, friends, family and community life. From PTA to Politics my mother was involved. One of my favorite memories was the yearly Toys for Tots drive. Every year, around Christmas, we went through all our toys, made piles, and bagged them according to category, i.e. stuffed animals, puzzles, games. We also bought new games for the needy children we personally sponsored. On the big day, we schlepped all our treasures to the community center and met the children we sponsored. In just a couple hours, the fun ended. But the lessons learned about caring, sharing and sacrifice were eternal.

This is the America I grew up in. Whatever the need, mom was there. Time and time again I watched my mother sacrifice the little she had for those who needed it more.

My mother taught me what it truly meant to be an American.

A PERSONAL NOTE . . .

ℬ

When someone touches something I passionately love, which in this case is the United States of America, I cannot be silent.

This book started with a question I received from my dear friend, Larry Cote:

Hi Kim, just wanted to get your take on Donald Trump, it looks like he will be the Republican nominee, is this a good thing, if so why? A lot of people here are torn, they don't like Hillary or the Democrats but, were hoping for someone better than Donald to be the change we were hoping for after 8 years of Obama.

I always value your opinion and knowledge.

Thank You, Larry

In response, I wrote a brief paragraph as to why I knew he would be the Republican nominee and ended with this statement:

As for other issues, such as character, repentance remarks, policy, women, immigration, Israel, trade and everything else the media, GOP, and Conservatives challenge him on, I will discuss in a separate letter.

Well, here is the separate letter—200 plus pages later. What started out as a letter to clarify the character and position statements of then President elect Donald Trump, turned into a book about that which is working in the shadows to undermine the foundations of America. All of which showed its ugly head when Trump decided to run for Office.

During the tireless effort exerted to write and publish this book before the November 8 election, I came to realize that this manuscript was being written for the days, weeks, months and even years following the election. Why? First, because the initial research of a what started out as a few issues became startlingly expansive—like the bottomless pit of hell. Secondly, the book addresses crucial issues that cannot be ignored by Americans or elected officials if America is to survive as a leading democracy.

With that said, the content contained herein is as unique as the 2015-2016 election cycle itself. Furthermore, these pages reflect my belief that the G-D of Abraham, Isaac, and Jacob, oversees the affairs of men and women on the earth. He raises up leaders and He sets them down. He hides things and reveals things. And because of such, I believe He still speaks to individuals, societies, governments and nations. Hence, I trust He is speaking throughout this book.

There are insights contained within these pages that are, G-D revelations. Daniel wrote about G-D in this manner, "He reveals the deep and secret things: He knows what is in the darkness, and the light dwells with him."[1]

What you are about to read concerns the deep and secret things—that which is obscure to the human eye. These secret things do belong to the L-RD, but once revealed they belong to us. And what we do with what's revealed is up to us—Do we make America Great Again, or do we redefine America to fit a different mold?

In closing, allow me to share the scripted words M (Dame Judi Dench) used to defend the British Secret Service in her last James Bond movie, Skyfall. These words succinctly describe what I came to understand while writing *Unraveling the Washington Web*.

I suppose that I see a different world than you do, and the truth is that what I see frightens me. I am frightened because our enemies are no longer known to us. They do not exist on a map, they're not nations, they are individuals. Look around you, who do you fear? Can you see a face, a uniform, a flag? No. Our world is not more transparent now, it's more opaque. It's in the shadows. That's where we must do battle.

I have one more thing to say. Here, today, I remember this which I think is from Tennyson, "we are not now that strength which in old days moved earth and heaven. That which we are, we are. One equal temper of heroic hearts made weak by time and fate, but strong in will to strive, to seek, to find and not to yield."

৪৩

FOREWORD

by Bill Mehlman

৪০

Kim Johnson has given us in these pages an MRI of a U.S. Constitution on the cusp of free fall. Its precarious condition recalls Benjamin Franklin's prophetic reply to the question "What have we created here?" posed to him by a concerned observer at the close of the Constitutional Convention in Philadelphia in 1787. "A republic," Franklin replied, "if we can keep it."

For the better part of two-plus centuries, in war and in peace, in good times and bad, we have managed to keep it, this constitutional anchor to which our rights and responsibilities are indispensably linked. Even in our worst moments it has stood as an impenetrable shield against any threat to the collegial but equal and independent executive, legislative and judicial powers that have charted America's course. Mistakes along the way were inevitable, but the organic structure of the document produced in Philadelphia by the most remarkable group of men ever to create a nation, always kept the gate open to course correction.

We have witnessed over nearly two decades and most pointedly in the last eight years, an erosion of the concept of divided decision-making powers unprecedented in American history, compounded by a politicization of virtually every aspect of the nation's social and civil marketplace. They are in evidence wherever one looks, most prominently in the widespread displacement of the federal legislative process by executive decree; in an open-borders immigration stance that has made a mockery of national sovereignty; in the admission to our shores of hundreds of thousands of poorly vetted and virtually un-vetted immigrants from countries culturally prone to violence, and in the suspicion of whole government agencies being manipulated for political advantage.

On the social-civil side of the ledger we have witnessed what can only be called an unholy alliance between the mainstream Protestant religious establishment and a political party wedded to abortion on demand, delusionary gender concepts, race obsession, income redistribution, confiscatory, job-killing taxation and a continued American retreat from its role as guardian of international peace and stability. The cure for these ills are in the hands of the American people. As they sow, so shall they reap. But if it is the most lucid, measured portrayal of the challenges to their constitutional democracy they seek, they will find it in this brilliant exposition by historian Kim Johnson.

ଛ

When the leaders choose to make themselves bidders at an auction of popularity, their talents, in the construction of the state, will be of no service. They will become flatterers instead of legislators; the instruments, not the guides, of the people.

Edmund Burke

℘

CHAPTER ONE

Spider webs, Cockatrice Eggs, and Vipers

"None calls for justice, nor any pleads for truth: they trust in vanity, and speak lies; they conceive mischief, and bring forth iniquity. They hatch cockatrice' eggs, and weave the spider's web: he that eats of their eggs dies, and that which is crushed breaks out into a viper."

Isaiah 59:4-5

&

Whether it's the latest James Bond movie Spectre, or the most recent House of Cards episode, there is one thing for certain; you are watching webs of unfathomable evil being spun and unraveled. Let's face it. The bad guys of today aren't the bad guys of the 1960's, 70's or 80's. Today, they are narcissistic liars and master manipulators of everything evil. They make the villains in Dudley Do-Right look like saints.

If you have ever watched the House of Cards, even one episode, you understand that deep gnawing feeling in the pit of your stomach that screams—I am watching some bad stuff—real evil. And as the plot thickens you might ask questions like, "does this really happen in Washington? Can one or two individuals wield that much power? And if so, how?"

Now, let's turn our attention to the movie Spectre which boasts the following synopsis:

A cryptic message from Bond's past sends him on a trail to Mexico City and Rome where he infiltrates a secret meeting and uncovers the existence of the sinister organization, Spectre. While M battles political forces to keep the secret service alive, Bond peels back the layers of deceit to untangle the web and reveal the chilling truth behind Spectre.

From Mexico to Rome, the web was spun. And the more visible it became, the more Bond realized that it was all encompassing—entangling everyone Spectre touched. Only truth could destroy the web, but to reach the truth, there had to be a reckoning with the past and a disdain for the present.

Think about it. Two fictional stories with plots utilizing the imagery of the spider web—spinning and capturing its victims in obscurity; unseen and most importantly, invisible to the public eye. How the web is spun is masterfully portrayed in the House of Cards and how the web is unraveled is painstakingly revealed in the movie Spectre.

That's fiction—thrilling, edge of your seat fiction.

Yet, what the American people and the world witnessed throughout the 2016 election campaign unto the present, is not fiction. From Mexico to Rome, the White House to the Kremlin—it's real. And you've had a spectacular front and center seat to Washington's web of evil.

So how did we get here? What is *really* going on behind the scenes in Washington? And how could a businessman like Donald Trump rise to become President of the United States?

ॐ

Cockatrice Eggs

For years, I've pondered the following verse from Isaiah 59:5, "they hatch cockatrice' eggs, and weave the spider's web: he that eats of their eggs dies, and that which is crushed breaks out into a viper." Yet, it was not until Donald Trump began to challenge the Washington status quo and the global political elites, that I understood what the prophet was trying to tell us. I say, *"tell us"* because we are the recipients of scripture's wisdom and its historical lessons. One who learns from them is one who can change the future.

The context surrounding Isaiah's metaphor describes Israel's political and spiritual condition before the Babylonian exile. The nation had reached a state of lawlessness that left no other option than Divine intervention; a course correction directed by God, Himself. A pattern dually noted throughout Israel's history.

Isaiah 59 begins with Isaiah telling the people that the LORD's hand is still outstretched, and His ear can still hear. In other words, God had not moved, and all His senses were working perfectly. He was still in their midst. Who had moved away from God, though, was Israel. Her sins and iniquities seriously impeded her relationship with the Almighty. As a nation, her hands were defiled with the blood of heinous crimes. Her lips knew nothing but lies and her tongue spoke perversely. At the root of Israel's unruliness was the absence of two important pillars of society: *justice and truth.* And without those two supports center stage in the consciousness of the nation, the political elites were having a field day. The list of their transgressions was endless; from the shedding of innocent blood to the destruction of the Torah's (law) moral foundation. They pretended to want peace, but instead they incited violence. Isaiah summed up their actions with these words "there is no judgment in their endeavors, and all their paths are crooked."[2]

Why was there no judgment? Because there was no truth. Hear what God said, "And judgment is turned away backward, and justice stands afar off: for truth is fallen in the street, and equity cannot enter. Yes, truth fails; and he that departs from evil becomes a prey: and the LORD saw it, and it displeased him that there was no judgment."[3]

When a nation loses its judgment—it can no longer find its way. It cannot discern between right and wrong, good and evil, holy and perverse. It may have an abundance of help from maps to navigational apps, motivational speakers to psychologists, but when it comes to everyday life, its people are lost.

Judgment is not the same as "judging." It is the ability to make sound decisions amidst conflicting circumstances. You may remember the story of King Solomon who had to judge between two mothers and one baby. In brief, the story goes like this: There were two mothers who bore children at the same time. One night, one of the mothers smothered her baby while sleeping. So, she slipped into the room of the other mother and exchanged her dead child for the living one. In the morning when they awoke, the mother of the living child knew that the dead child was not her baby, but the other mother insisted it was. Hence, the matter was brought to the king. He heard their stories and proclaimed, "Divide the living child in two, and give half to the one, and half to the other." Immediately, the real birth mother cried out telling him to give the living child to the other woman. But the murdering mother cried, "no, divide it, let it not be mine or hers." Then Solomon commanded that the living child be given to its true birth mother. How wise was that—I mean he went to the source of truth, the heart. Is it not written that "out of the abundance of the heart the mouth speaks?" This is an example of wise judgment—rightly dividing between the truth and the lie and providing a solution for the problem.

What struck me, and apparently, millions of other Americans, when Donald Trump first stepped into the political arena was his ability to look through the smokescreen of the Washington elites and bring solution based ideas to America's challenges. Yes, his rhetoric was crass, and yes, his speech was simple (for some, too simple), but his tongue was sharp like a sword exposing and unraveling the Washington web, one strand at a time.

It was the aftermath of Trump's first campaign appearance that caused me to have an "aha moment" over Isaiah's spider webs and cockatrice eggs. My years of pondering were over. What happened? Trump stepped on a cockatrice egg. Have you ever heard of a cockatrice egg?

Isaiah said that political elites who reject justice and judgment hatch them. What are they? They, my friends, are the eggs of poisonous serpents like the death adder or the viper that thrust out their tongues to kill their victims. The word "cockatrice" comes from the Hebrew root word, "צֶפַע (tseh'fah)" which means, "to extrude."

In fact, did you know that the death adder has the most highly developed venom-injecting mechanism of all snakes? Interestingly, they are not aggressive animals. They only inject venom when they are threatened, caught or stepped on[4] Furthermore, the death adder doesn't hunt its prey, but lies in ambush and draws its prey to it. A death adder can go from strike position, to strike and envenoming its prey, and back to strike position in less than 0.15 seconds—that's less than 1/4 of a second.[5]

Did you happen to notice what happened within hours and days after Trump exposed the corruption of the Mexican government during his June 16th campaign announcement? Macy's dropped his clothing line, NBC and Univision (Spanish broadcaster) dropped the Ms. Universe and Ms. USA pageants,[6] and Serta dropped his mattress line. Then ESPN and NASCAR had their moment: ESPN pulled out of a golf outing at Trump National Golf Club in Los Angeles, and NASCAR reneged on a banquet scheduled at the Trump National Miami Doral resort.

Yes, Donald Trump stepped on one or two Washington cockatrice eggs and out came the vipers.

Macy's, pressured by the organization MoveOn.org, told MSNBC, "In light of statements made by Donald Trump, which is inconsistent with Macy's values, we have decided to discontinue our business relationship with Mr. Trump . . .." Serta's rationale was, "Serta values diversity and does not agree with nor endorse the recent statements made by Mr. Trump." NBC said, "At NBC, respect, and dignity for all people are cornerstones of our values. Due to the recent derogatory statements by Donald Trump regarding immigrants, NBC Universal is ending its business relationship with Mr. Trump."[7]

As for ESPN and NASCAR they just flowed with the politically correct wave of human rights.

About all of them Trump wrote:

I have lost a lot during this Presidential run defending the people of the United States. I have always heard that it is very hard for a successful person to run for President. Macy's, NBC, Serta, and NASCAR have all taken the weak and very sad position of being politically correct even though they are wrong in terms of what is good for our country. [8]

Notably these companies are all American born, so their acts of disavowing Donald Trump over his immigration comments, in a country of free speech, leads us to ask, "what was taking place behind the scenes?"

Let's start with Macy's.

MoveOn.org created a petition to intimidate Macy's into disenfranchising Trump. The petition read:

Macy's: Donald Trump does not reflect "the magic of Macy's." We urge you to sever ties with him. Macy's says it has a strong obligation to be "socially responsible" and that "actions speak louder than words." Indeed, it's time to act.[9]

Comparing Macy's lack of response to that of NBC's quick response, the petition released its adder's venom into its unsuspecting signee. It was a vilification of Trump to the first degree! Hatred framed in such a way to make both Trump and Macy's look like full-fledged enemies of social responsibility.

Before we move beyond Macy's and into the heart of the Washington web could there be anything menacing about MoveOn.org?

Well, as a matter of fact, yes. Infowars.com noted that, "The group acts as a front for wealthy Democrats. It was founded with the help of financier George Soros who donated $1.46 million to get the organization rolling. Linda Pritzker of the Hyatt hotel family also gave the group a $4 million donation."[10] Additionally, MoveOn.org has a serious problem with telling the truth. FactCheck.org dually noted that the organization has misled the public numerous times particularly during election campaigns.

Do you remember MoveOn.org's Fat Cat TV AD that played during the Obama—Romney race? It flaunted a few cute and cuddly fat cats while sending this subliminal message: "when the wealthiest 1% pay a fair tax rate like the rest of us, it keeps the American dream alive for everyone." Sounds just, doesn't it? Well, MoveOn.org wanted you to believe those fat cats were millionaires and billionaires who were not paying their fair share. Yet, based upon the statistics used by MoveOn.org, those fat cats were neither billionaires nor millionaires; they were the 1 million American households earning around $500,000. And, per FactCheck, this 1% was paying 10-20% more in income taxes than the "rest of us." Wouldn't you agree that MoveOn.org's use of cute and cuddly fat cats to deceive and manipulate the American people was dishonest?[11]

Another organization that has issues with MoveOn.org is PolitiFact.com. PolitiFact.com has their famous Truth-O-Meter showing that only 36% of MoveOn's statements are accurate. The other 64% register half-truths or false; falling close to the red buzzer that sets off the siren shouting, "Liar, liar, your pants are on fire."[12] All of that's bad, but bad becomes sinister when funding comes from America's number one subversionist, George Soros. MoveOn.org is one of Washington's cockatrice eggs.

Most people I speak with are not familiar with George Soros, so let's spend the remainder of this chapter looking at a key figure behind the Washington web and more than a few cockatrice eggs.

಄

Meet George Soros

If you are a Glenn Beck fan or a politico, then you've probably heard of George Soros, otherwise doubtful. You need to know who he is because he is in the shadows weaving the Washington web. With that said, he's not a patriotic American. In fact, he makes Frances Underwood, the evil, sadistic, power player in House of Cards look like the face of innocence.

You may not know Soros, but you sure can recognize him. Under the Obama administration, Soros left his imprint all over the country and of late, continues to do so. Interestingly, throughout the 2016 campaign, whenever there was a ridiculous outburst of protest in our nation, you can believe Soros was behind it—whether it was Occupy Wall Street, Black Lives Matter, or Dump Trump. Even now, over a year into the Trump administration his fingerprints linger with agendas like unseat President Trump, ANTIFA gatherings, and the Russian collusion dossier.[13]

So, who is he? If you google him, your first read will be George Soros is a Hungarian-American business magnate, investor, political activist and an author who is of Jewish-Hungarian ancestry and holds dual citizenship. He is chairman of Soros Fund Management." And then you might see another bio that reads, "George Soros was born in Budapest, Hungary on August 12, 1930. After surviving the Nazi invasion and occupation of Hungary in the early 1940s, Soros fled the then-Communist-dominated Hungary in 1947 and made his way to England."

Both bio's make George Soros out to be a Hungarian Jew that survived the Holocaust and afterward forged a new life in England—very misleading, very misleading indeed. Yes, George Soros is both a Hungarian Jew and a Holocaust survivor, but how he survived the Holocaust is another story. At the age of thirteen, George posed as the godson of an official within Hungary's fascist government. His first job was that of a Judenrat—one who snitched on Jews.[1415] His second job involved accompanying and at times aiding his Nazi godfather in confiscating Jewish wealth. Concerning this phase of his life Soros declared, "this was when my character was made."[16] A very telling statement.

When Soros was 14 years old, his wealthy father, "bribed a government official to take 14-year-old George in and swear that he was his Christian godson."[17] That's understandable as a good father would do anything to ensure the safety of his family. So, who was the Nazi that his father bribed? Bambach, a Hungarian official who directly or indirectly reported to Francois Genoud, the Reich's treasury keeper. During the war, Bambach took George with him to confiscate Jewish property which, in turn, allegedly connected him to Genoud. How or when George became connected to Genoud is unclear. What is known is that they became lifelong friends.

During the war, Francois Genoud met and funded Amin al-Husseini, the Grand Mufti of Jerusalem, under Hitler's orders. After the war, he managed the hidden Nazi treasury and funded the defense of many Nazis'.[18] He also admitted being the conspirator of the Palestinian hijacking of the Belgian Sabena Airlines Flight 571, as it flew from Vienna to Tel Aviv, on May 8, 1972. He became the founder of the Arab Commercial Bank of Switzerland used to fund terrorism operations, of which Pamela Geller says, "he may have even started his bank with the Nazi treasure that was stolen goods and gold from the Jews."[19] And if that's not enough to make your jaw drop, he is on printed record saying that, "Hitler wanted the movement to move from Nazism to Islamism and to carry on the National Socialism movement to gain control of the world and to exterminate Jews."[20] This is a man who influenced George Soros and helped shape his character. And notably, Soros likes to deal with people who oversee treasuries; first, Francois Genoud and secondly, former U.S. Secretary of the Treasury, Jack Lew—coincidence?

In May of 2015, days after Soros warned Washington to succumb to China on the IMF currency basket, he was hacked by CyberBerkut. The hack exposed confidential email correspondence between Soros and Ukrainian President, Petro Poroshenko. In one email, Soros laid out a strategy for the Ukraine to obtain a much-needed $15 billion in financial support from the European Union (EU). He concluded the email as follows:

> Based on that commitment, the Federal Reserve could be asked to extend a $15 billion three-month swap arrangement with the National Bank of Ukraine. That

would reassure the markets and avoid a panic. . ..If you do, you would have to call Chancellor Merkel to ask for a commitment in principle to the $15 billion package. I am ready to call Jack Lew of the US Treasury to sound him out about the swap agreement.[21]

Call Jack Lew of the U.S. Treasury? Since when does a business man call the U.S. Treasury for funds to support a foreign country, even if it is an ally? Since never, so how could Soros have that kind of influence? Possibly because he was bank rolling the Obama administration in hopes that Obama would further his European vision expressed during a ValueWalks speech:[22]

"The European Union was a very inspiring idea to people like me." Reflecting back to when European economies were more balanced, "It was the embodiment of the concept of an Open Society, like-minded countries getting together and sacrificing part of their sovereignty for the common good. It was meant to be a voluntary association of equals."[23]

It's important to note the term "Open Society" in Soros' speech. There is a direct connection between this term and his vision as represented by his philanthropic organization, *the Open Society Foundation.*

The Open Society Foundation (OSF) is a U.S. based humanitarian NGO with far-reaching implications, of which I've already touched upon with MoveOn.org.

Furthermore, OSF has close ties with U.S. Institutions such as USAID.

According to Global Research,

> USAID, working with billionaire George Soros' Open Society, also funds the Organized Crime and Corruption Reporting Project, which engages in 'investigative journalism' that usually goes after governments that have fallen into disfavor with the United States and then are singled out for accusations of corruption. The USAID-funded OCCRP also collaborates with Bellingcat, an online investigative website founded by blogger Eliot Higgins.[24]

OSF also uses incitement to further its "so-called" social justice agendas. For example, it is a well-known fact that George Soros, through the Open Society Foundation, funded a base of activist groups to mobilize Ferguson protests. How much did he donate? Thirty-three million dollars. And this is social justice? According to the Daily Mail, "Liberal billionaire George Soros donated $33 million to social justice organizations which helped turn events in Ferguson from a local protest into a national flashpoint."[25] In the words of the Washington Times,

> "Its liberal billionaire George Soros, who has built a business empire that dominates across the ocean in Europe while forging a political machine powered by nonprofit foundations that impact American politics and policy, not unlike what he did with MoveOn.org."

And "Mr. Soros gave at least $33 million in one year to support already-established groups that emboldened the grass-roots, on-the-ground activists in Ferguson, according to the most recent tax filings of his nonprofit Open Society Foundations."[26]

In summary, George Soros used the Ferguson shooting to turn a "one-day criminal event in Missouri into a 24-hour-a-day national cause for celebration."[27] Tell me, how did this help the Ferguson community? How did this work towards justice on behalf of Michael Brown or Officer Darren Wilson? And how did it foster reconciliation and peace making on any level?

What is truly sad is that Mr. Soros and his Open Society Foundation are not furthering a better America. Instead, they are injecting the viper's venom into American Society by trashing American justice and its values while playing the human rights race card in the name of "social justice."

Today, in America, social justice trends that equate "race and color to everything just" are being fomented. Hence, if a minority (legal or illegal) commits a crime or assaults a police officer he or she is viewed as the "just" victim and the non-minority citizen (regardless of race) and the officer is looked upon as the "unjust" perpetrator. No more is breaking the law regarded as "breaking the law." It is propagandized with a racial bias that says, "if a minority is arrested for a crime it is because the majority community is racist." Nothing could be farther from the truth, in most cases. Therefore, it's important to clarify that being a minority is not a crime, but breaking the law is. This distinction must not be distorted for any sect of American society, including government elites.

Unethical and illegal behavior needs to remain the demarcation line for justice and judgment. This does not mean that every crime is worthy of a jail sentence or a punishment, but it does say that we must call bad—wrong and good—right; no more blurring the lines. If we choose not to be law abiding citizens, then surely what Isaiah said about "justice and judgment being turned back" will be a truism of America.

How do we change this trend? With "teshuva, [28] repentance"—doing an about-face and returning to God's human rights laws as the basis of American social justice.

With that said, I would be remiss not to mention that George Soros was behind the Panama Papers scandal. If the above isn't enough to make you think twice about why Donald Trump has been so outspoken on American identity, issues and values, then let's take one more look into Soros' far-reaching control under the Obama administration.

The Panama Paper Scandal leak was initiated by *International Consortium of Investigative Journalists (ICIJ)*, funded by none other than George Soros and the

Open Society Foundation. About the ICIJ you might find the following statement of interest:

> The United States Center for Public Integrity and the International Consortium of Investigative Journalists participate in a multi-year media war, which Soros launched against the Koch brothers, billionaires associated with right-wing Republican circles. Periodically, during the campaign, Soros' journalists were convicted of outright fraud, violating U.S. law, and distorting facts.[29]

Another player in the Panama Paper leaks was the Ford Foundation. According to Hang the Bankers, "The Ford Foundation is connected to the CIA and has specialized in international cultural propaganda since the end of the Second World War." Henry Ford was also involved in Nazi propaganda here in the United States during World War II, and he even received an award called the *Adolf Hitler Award*. Did you know Ford was honored by the Nazis?

Furthermore, I sat down with the author of the May 2016, NGO Monitor's UNOCHA-oPt (United Nations Office for the Coordination of Humanitarian Affairs) report. The report's findings revealed extensive manipulation of data by the UN used to delegitimize Israel. Within the document, numerous NGO's (non-governmental organizations) and their acts to delegitimize Israel, are mentioned. I discussed the findings with the author and expressed my surprise of the Ford

Foundation's involvement; only to later learn that both the Ford Foundation and the Open Society Foundation are directly and indirectly funding most anti-Israel NGO's.

With that said, the Panama Paper leaks apparently had a geopolitical agenda. All the elites mentioned in the scandal, of which Vladimir Putin was at the top, are not only the opponents of George Soros but also the geopolitical enemies of the U.S. State Department. [30] According to the editor of the Event Chronicles,

> The offshore scandal is the result of a public-private partnership. All persons involved are Soros' opponents, but when they are also the geopolitical enemies of the U.S., the most serious charges are put forward. . .. Liberal left figures associated with Soros himself, who actively use offshore companies for financial speculation, do not appear anywhere on the lists. [31]

The Panama Paper scandal leads us right back to where we started, the connection of George Soros to the U.S. Treasury and other governmental organizations including, but not limited to, the CIA and the U.S. State Department. By August of 2010, there were already reports that Soros had allegedly visited the White House 35 times. [32][33] He not only met with then President Obama, but also with a man named Rob Malley.

Who is Rob Malley? Robert Malley was special assistant to President Obama on the National Security

Council (NSC), a senior advisor to the president for the counter-ISIL campaign, and the White House coordinator for the Middle East, North Africa, and Persian Gulf region.[34] He was often referred to as Obama's ISIL Czar. But before becoming a senior National Security advisor, he served as the Middle East and North Africa Program Director of the Soros-funded International Crisis Group.[35] Furthermore, Malley has an interesting family background, one that undoubtedly has created some strong anti-democratic pro-Marxist biases. Notably, his family is vehemently anti-Israel and boasts of having been good friends with Yasser Arafat.[36] That makes sense when you learn that his parents started the Egyptian Communist Party and later were kicked out of France for their radical views and threats to chiefs of state. What's that adage, "Birds of a feather flock together?"

Are you beginning to see how deep the Washington web goes and how many cockatrice eggs are lying around? Are you starting to see what Donald Trump was up against during his election campaign? And, why that every time he mentioned a problem within Washington, he stepped on a cockatrice egg and out came a viper?

I'm almost done talking about Soros. Do you have any questions? Would you like to know how much money he poured into Hillary's campaign? Or how he manipulates European election outcomes? The figures documented to date show that Soros donated over 8 million to Hillary's campaign[37] and over 25 million to Democratic candidates.

In addition to Hillary, her running mate Senator Tim Kaine, held a private dinner with Soros' son, Alexander—another top tier financier of the Democratic party. DC Leaks has exposed Soros for using his NGO's to manipulate European elections.[38]

Thankfully, Soros and all his money couldn't buy the American people in this election—he didn't win and hopefully never will.

As we segue into chapter two and back to the issues behind Trump's campaign and the unraveling of the Washington Web, let me say one last thing about George Soros, "he has an acute messianic complex." In 2004, the L.A. Times penned the following:

"America, under Bush, is a danger to the world," says Soros. To save the world and prevent the reelection of George W. Bush, Soros has dedicated extraordinary amounts of time and money because defeating Bush, he says, is his "central focus." His motto, "If I spend enough, I will make it right," is the essence of his articulated ideas about changing society. "I do not accept the rules imposed by others. . .. And in periods of regime change, the normal rules don't apply. . .. If truth be known, I carried some rather potent messianic fantasies with me from childhood, which I felt I had to control, otherwise they might get me in trouble. . .. Next to my fantasies about being God, I also have very strong fantasies of being mad," Soros once confided on British television."[39]

At times throughout the election campaign, I wondered if Trump wasn't running against Soros—two Billionaires dueling it out for America's honor. Who knew that when Trump called out illegal immigration, unprotected borders, and corruption within the Mexican Government, that he would step on not just one cockatrice egg, but a whole nest! And inevitably, out came the adders and the vipers striking with precision and recoiling as if nothing happened.

Was Trump's position statement on Mexico and immigration a valid issue to his campaign and the subsequent immigration battle? Is there as big of a problem as he insisted there is? And if so, what solutions could Trump provide for America? Let's find out.

℘

CHAPTER TWO

Legal or Illegal?

"One law shall be to him that is home born, and unto the stranger that sojourns among you." Exodus 12:49

&

As Americans, whether you are conservative or liberal, immigration is at the heart of who we are—a nation of immigrants. Whether it's our founding fathers who sought freedom from religious oppression and tyranny or our masses who fled Europe pre-and post-Holocaust, or our Mexican and South American immigrants escaping poverty, or our Syrian refugees escaping death, one thing is forever settled in the American collective conscience—they are welcome in America.

For the world, America is a place of hope, a place where their world can change and where they can change the world. So, what's the problem?

The eight years, prior to the Trump administration, gave rise to serious immigration issues, of which the word "illegal" was center stage. And yet, although illegal immigration was at the forefront of political debates, it was not until Trump linked Mexico and Mexicans with "crime, drug cartels, rape and murder" that the whole debate erupted into a violent mass media race-bashing frenzy. On June 16th, 2015 when Trump announced his run for President he noted issues that would be addressed in his candidacy—and at the top was the cockatrice egg: Illegal Immigration. And when he stepped on it—out came a viper.

Here is an excerpt from his speech:

When do we beat Mexico at the border? They're laughing at us, at our stupidity. And now they are beating us economically. They are not our friend, believe me. But they're killing us economically. The U.S. has become a dumping ground for everybody else's problems. (Applause)

Thank you. It's true, and these are the best and the finest. When Mexico sends its people, they're not sending their best. They're not sending you. They're not sending you. They're sending people that have lots of problems, and they're bringing those problems with them. They're bringing drugs. They're bringing crime. They're rapists. And some, I assume, are good people. But I speak to border guards, and they tell us what we're getting. And it only makes common sense. It only makes common sense. They're not sending us the right people.

It's coming from more than Mexico. It's coming from all over South and Latin America, and it's coming probably — probably — from the Middle East. But we don't know. Because we have no protection and we have no competence, we don't know what's happening. And it's got to stop, and it's got to stop fast.

Notably, weeks after Donald Trump's scathing assessment of how the Mexican government was sending murderers and rapists, Kate Steinle, a thirty-two-year-old woman, was murdered by an illegal Mexican immigrant, Juan Francisco Lopez-Sanchez, on San Francisco Pier 14, July of 2015.

Bill O'Reilly took the killing of Kate Steinle, very seriously and tied it into his Talking Points Memo entitled, "The Vilification of Donald Trump."

He pointed out that Donald Trump was correct in his assessment of the border situation but could have been more articulate and precise in the way he portrayed Mexico and Mexican illegals—because, he said, most illegals are good law-abiding citizens, and they do not fall into the category of murderers and rapists (of which I wholeheartedly agree).

In his Talking Points Memo, he referred to the 1996, "Illegal Immigration Reform and Responsibility Act (IIRIRA)" that Bill Clinton signed into law. This act made it clear that "local and state authorities were to cooperate with the Federal Government in apprehending illegals, especially illegal criminals." Time and time again, illegal criminals were given a pass and often found living in sanctuary cities that would not deport or imprison them.

Concerning Kate Steinle, O'Reilly rightly condemned the establishment's response to San Francisco's violation of the law and dually noted that, "Racial politics drives the law these days, which is why Trump caught so much hell. The Constitution demands that the Federal Government protects the American people from foreign intruders—it demands it." He continues, "Obviously, that responsibility is not being met. But if you point that out, as Mr. Trump did, you are a racist. A piñata for the border crowd to bash."

Bill O'Reilly acted and developed Kate's Law. How did the Latino community respond to it?

Samanta Honigman, an undergraduate student at New York University, wrote the following in her article entitled, "Kate's Law and the License to Hate."[40]

"Kate's Law" addresses what is really a bureaucratic problem with a nuclear bomb. Sections of "Kate's

Law" actually create stricter punishments, a legal double standard, for all undocumented immigrants. In fact, as you can see from page 3 on BillCam, the bill gives people without papers much harsher sentences for the same offense than someone with papers would receive. Surely this violates the section of the 14th Amendment that ensures due process of law for all persons, regardless of immigration status.

If that doesn't make you want to pull your hair out, I don't know what does. What she just said was, "an illegal immigrant has the same rights as a legal immigrant and therefore, has a right to due process of law." When I worked for Jewish Vocational Services, I taught immigrants and underprivileged women office skills for placement into the workplace. I had a sign spanning my entire blackboard that read "what don't you understand about the word, NO?" You would understand why if you had my students. Today, the banner would read "what don't you understand about the word, ILLEGAL?"

With that said, as Americans, we need leadership that will take the revamping of our immigration process seriously. It's apparent that we need new laws and a legal system that will streamline citizenship for those who are vetted, and legislation that helps to vet those who are illegal. We need to consider permanently deporting all illegals who commit crimes. We should not spend one more dollar holding them in our prisons. And, we should make it clear to every foreign government that if we catch

one of their citizens committing a crime in our country—
they will be deported, and you will pay all fees including
the airfare for their deportation. Also, they should never
be allowed back into our country—ever. Why? Because
they did not respect the opportunity availed to them. And
because deterrence is the best way to minimize crime,
illegal immigration, and terrorism.

This brings us to the issue of "entitlement."

൭

Entitled or Entitlement?

Under the Obama administration, there was an
ideological shift in the way Americans think. The tenets of
the European Union, the United Nations Human Rights
Council, decentralized market globalization, and the
blurring of all moral lines sadly gave way to an
"entitlement" mentality within our society. And this sense
of "entitlement" made its way into the immigration
narrative; particularly among those who migrate from
South American, Mexican, and Muslim societies. During
the Obama administration, the philosophy of entitlement
burgeoned throughout all economic and social classes.
Instead of legally striving for the American Dream, social
justice movements encouraged illegal immigrants to reach
for American entitlement—a lawless, unethical and
destructive ideal that rewards illegals and punishes hard-
working American citizens. Of late, California voted to

allow illegals Driver's Licenses which in turn gives them voting rights—are you ok with that?

It appears that Obama's idea of entitlement was that illegal immigrants or refugees are "entitled" to all our benefits without having to "obey" any of our laws. And, if you don't like our laws—such as the Secure Communities Act or the Illegal Immigration Reform and Responsibility Act (IIRIRA), then we will either change them or get rid of them.

Former President Obama lived in Eurotopia—let's dispense with accountability, borders, a constitution, the American dream and above all "justice and judgment" and join the human rights cesspool of tolerance, hypocrisy, immoral equivalence, injustice, and over-regulated European Union utopia.

If you think that is an exaggeration of his administration's views on immigration, keep reading.

Illegal immigrants have come to believe that it is not illegal to be illegal. They feel that if their country is suffering economically, experiencing gang violence, or being oppressed by a ruthless dictator, then it is our responsibility to help them. And the process to be a legal immigrant is, well, just too difficult.

According to Samanta Honigman,

Few of us would wait for the United States to process a visa over the course of many years if our families just over the border were in continual danger. One might ask, why can't Latino immigrants all just go through the process of securing citizenship? But few understand that applying for permanent residence and citizenship is a timely, expensive and arduous process, and it is out of reach for those who suffer the most economically. Sometimes, decent people feel that there is little other option for them but to live, at least for a while, under the radar.

Very few people do understand Samanta, why you and some in the Latino community feel that our process of immigration is "out of reach" for your human rights problems. And this is precisely what Trump is driving at—equity for legal American citizens does not include entitlement for illegal-American citizens.

So, how did "entitlement" become part of our immigrant "belief system?"

Let's return to the 1996 "Illegal Immigration Reform and Responsibility Act (IIRIRA)"—the hidden part.

Within the 1996 IIRIRA was a framework for establishing a National Identification System for Americans. The structure consisted of "three identification systems" that were offered to states as "test pilots." The provision provided $5 million-per-year grants to any State that would participate in one of the three pilot ID programs. And you may ask, why would that be important to our discussion on immigration? Because one of those programs was the "Criminal Alien Identification Program." This ID program was to link the fingerprint records of previously arrested aliens with the federal, state and local law enforcement agencies.

∞

Secure Communities to the Dream Act

Fast forward to 2009 when the program morphed into what became known as Secure Communities.[41] It was managed by the U.S. Immigration and Customs Enforcement (ICE), Interior Immigration, and the Department of Homeland Security.

Julia Preston wrote in her New York Times article dated November 12, 2009, that the Federal authorities have identified more than 111,000 immigrants with criminal records:

> Among the immigrants identified through the program, known as Secure Communities, more than 111,000 had been charged with or convicted of the most serious crimes, including murder and rape, domestic security officials said Thursday. About 1,900 of those were deported.

She further stated that "about 100,000 of the detained immigrants identified through the system had been convicted of less serious crimes, ranging from burglary to traffic offenses."

John Morton of ICE stated that Secure Communities were "the future of immigration enforcement" because it "focuses our resources on identifying and removing the most serious criminal offenders first and foremost."[42]

The goals of Secure Communities, as outlined in a 2009 report to Congress, were to Identify, Prioritize, and Transform (IPT). *Identify* criminal aliens through modernized information sharing; *Prioritize* enforcement actions to ensure apprehension and removal of dangerous criminal aliens; and *Transform* criminal alien enforcement processes and systems to achieve lasting results."[43]

Wow! You can go ahead and say it! Since 2009 "we've come a long way, baby!" Did immigration crime rates drop significantly since Secure Communities were expanded under the Obama administration?

Before we continue discussing what happened with the Secure Communities, let's take note of some facts in Julia's article. First, in 2008 over 111,000 illegal immigrants were charged with serious crimes which included murder and rape! Secondly, over 100,000 had committed minor crimes like burglary. Sound familiar?

When Trump said that the crimes being committed by illegals ranged from theft to rape, was he lying? Was he exaggerating? What do you think? Do you think rape is a serious crime? And how dangerous is burglary? How threatening one perceives a criminal act to be, determines how vocal one will be when a crime is committed.

Apparently, President Trump believes these crimes are serious.

The Secure Communities project went through several transitions between 2009 and 2012 until it was finally abandoned in 2014. Most of the changes took place between 2011 and 2012, before Obama's second term re-election. He wanted the Latino vote and to obtain it he reneged and dissolved policies that directly affected the national security of the American people.

In 2012, the Congressional Hispanic Caucus requested the suspension of the deportation program because they found it to be based on "administrative authority only." Subsequently, Boston Mayor Thomas Menino reported that, "the program, contrary to its stated goal, is negatively impacting public safety" and "numerous immigrants have been deported after committing only minor traffic violations."[44]

Of those deported from Illinois through May 2011, by ICE's accounting, less than 22% were convicted of a serious crime, 75% were never convicted of a serious crime, and more than 21% were not convicted of any offense.

Furthermore, the AFL-CIO, an organization that represented 7,000 ICE officers, issued a no-confidence vote due to the discrepancy in documentation. The ICE officers noted that the number of non-criminal ICE deportees was highly overinflated stating that, "many offenders agreed to be deported if all charges were dropped and they returned to the category of non-criminal."[45][46] Also, the ICE internal reports revealed 90% of all ICE detainees were arrested by local authorities, yet the public report showed otherwise.[47] That was just part of their accusations. According to Chris Cane, President of the National ICE Council Union, who testified before Congress, "the government was ordering the agents not to enforce the law in order to comply with the President's re-election campaign priorities.[48][49]

Hence, enters the Dream Act—Obama's answer to the then "highly controversial" Secure Communities. It is important to note that Secure Communities became highly criticized by local authorities due to the additional costs of implementing the 48-hour detainee rule. Furthermore, State and local officials felt it was wrong to deport illegal immigrants who only had minor criminal infractions or no criminal record—this thinking deserves a station identification break. Since when are "illegal" immigrants defined by whether or not they committed a crime?

℘

The Dream Act

The Dream Act was enacted to repair any damaged relations between President Obama and the Latino voters. So, what exactly was the Dream Act offering?

For starters "prosecutorial discretion" which meant, reviews are done on a case-by-case basis, and, then, Secretary Napolitano would provide relief for the accused.

Individuals who qualified for aid could also be granted work permits. Furthermore, the new policy appeared to make deportation cases involving people with no significant criminal record, less likely.[50][51] Napolitano, who resigned in 2013, said that the administration's policy "will not alleviate the need for passage of the Dream Act or for larger reforms to our immigration laws."

By summer 2011, according to Dino Grandoni of the Atlantic Wire, Obama had reportedly deported 1,000,000 illegal Mexicans. But by the summer of 2012, deportations had trickled to a slow drip and in 2013 President Obama was making deals with the Mexican[52] and South American governments to ensure free passage, education, and welfare to illegals who cross our southern American borders.[53]

In November 2015, the Pew report put out their annual "5 Facts About Illegal Immigration in the U.S."[54] The five facts included an explanation on Obama's expanded deportation relief which was voted down by the Supreme Court on June 23, 2016. The Pew report noted that, in 2014, there were 11.3 million illegal immigrants in America making up 3-5% of our population. Of those 11.3 million, Mexican illegal immigrants made up 49% and collectively they accounted for over 5% of the American workforce. And sadly, 7% of students K-12 in our public schools have at least one illegal parent. These statistics are not only daunting, but they reaffirm the need for a reformed immigration process—and quickly.

Unfortunately, daunting turned into nightmarish by the minute. On June 29, 2016, President Obama met with Mexican President Nieto, and Canadian Prime Minister Trudeau, to discuss the Trans-Pacific Trade Agreement. You may recall earlier in the chapter that I mentioned Obama had a Eurotopia vision of America and the world. At the center of the trifecta amigo meeting was the idea of "no borders" between our countries. Let's be one big happy trade family. No borders. Your problems are my problems. We love the poor, and we are happy to support you, too!

Of course, Trump was central to the discussions and thankfully, neither Nieto or Trudeau was foolish enough to fall for Obama's bait. They sidestepped specific questions about Trump, saying they would gladly work with whoever was elected to lead the United States.

But Obama wasn't happy with their graceful evasion of condemning Trump. He pushed the immigration agenda saying, "whoever becomes president of the United States is going to have a deep, strong interest in having a strong relationship with Mexico. That's our neighbor, our friend, and one of our biggest trading partners. I think I've made myself clear, setting aside whatever the candidates are saying, that America is a nation of immigrants, that's our strength." Wait for it . . ..

"Unless you were one of the first Americans unless you are Native American, somebody, somewhere, in your past showed up from someplace else. And they didn't always have papers."[55]

Need I say more? . . .Yes.

೮౦

Arizona's Conundrum

To continue the subject of immigration, after what seems to be the perfect ending to the chapter, may seem a little excessive. So, if you need to take a five-minute break—do it now. As Paul Harvey would say, "Now, for the rest of the story." Hopefully, you'll find this next segment that leads to profiling of interest, and honestly, I don't want to lose you now.

You may remember the 2012 Supreme Court's ruling of Arizona's Immigration Laws?

There was a split decision by the Supreme Court, and the last three clauses were deemed unconstitutional. They revoked Arizona's rights to criminally penalize persons for seeking work, or for failing to register with the federal government. They stopped police from making warrantless arrests based upon suspicion of suspected illegal status and deport ability under the federal law. And they ensured that immigrants would not be required to carry national proof of their legal status.[56]

The only clause that remained was the "show me your papers" provision which allowed state law enforcement officials to check the immigration status of a person who was stopped or arrested; and only if they had reason to suspect him or her of being in the country illegally.[57]

Now, I am writing this book while attending school in Israel. On Friday afternoons before Shabbat (Friday evening to Saturday night), I often travel from Haifa to either Tel Aviv or Jerusalem to stay with friends. I pack a small overnight bag. As I approach the train station with my tiny overnight bag I am asked, in Hebrew, for my identification. I have to show the Security Guard my U.S. Passport, or I cannot travel—it's that simple. And that's within the country; I am not even crossing a border! Yet, in my own country, it is forbidden for law enforcement to check the identification of a foreigner. Members of drug cartels and terrorist networks along with law abiding citizens can cross state lines, set up shop, and nobody is the wiser. And there are those who think Trump is too vocal about this issue—what do you think?

Here is the final statement made by the Supreme Court regarding Arizona: "The State may not pursue policies that undermine Federal Law," and "detaining individuals solely to verify their immigration status would raise Constitutional concerns," wrote Justice Anthony Kennedy, expressing the majority opinion. Justice Antonin Scalia, of blessed memory, vocally objected not only to the majority argument in this case but also to the administration's immigration policies.[58]

By the time Obama took office in 2012, the 1996 "Illegal Immigration Reform and Responsibility Act (IIRIRA)" was dismantled. All immigration restrictions marginalized, and all security protocols minimized—and all in the name of "affirmative action" and "liberty."

And, as for making an example out of Arizona? Then President Obama expressed his fear that the ONE provision accepted by the court may lead to racial profiling.[59] So let's go there.

℥

What's Racial Profiling?

What is racial profiling? Why did President Obama hate it so much? How could it be used to keep Americans safe? And why is the Trump administration considering it? These are just a few questions that play a significant role in understanding how and why our National Security entities—from NSA to TSA struggle to be effective.

In 1968, my mother put me on a plane all by myself. I was eight years old when I received my first set of bronze wings from the Delta stewardess assigned to watch over me. That was many years ago. Since then I've been privileged to fly around the world, literally. I love to travel and explore this magnificent world God created, just for us. The world is full of beautiful people, rich and diverse cultures, spectacular scenery, life-giving wildernesses and just plain cool animals. And one of my favorite places to travel is, Israel.

But travel has changed, *really* changed since I was a little girl. Oh, how I loved the fancy flight wings I would receive from the stewardesses. And when it came to mealtime, which back then was included even on the shorter flights, I so enjoyed receiving a meal-tray with a quaint place setting of a china plate, vintage petite silverware, and a tea cup. Believe it or not, I still have my Finnish Air silverware from my first overseas flight from Chicago to the Soviet Union in 1977. And might I add, security was a breeze to go through. No need to take off your shoes or belts—remember? Why? It was not because there were no threats or that we were too lax. It was simply because, at that time we profiled; yep, National Security included profiling.

After 9/11 that all changed. Heightened security scares coupled with a political desire to abate attacks on innocent Muslim citizens wrought dramatic security changes. It started with shoes and it evolved into X-ray machines. I was living in Singapore at the time of 9/11 and I remember returning to a different America. Today, the only thing many of us have are wonderful memories of the way "it used to be."

Now, I had been traveling in and out of Israel for over ten years before 9/11. And going through Israeli security was no picnic, let me tell you. You never saw anyone mistreated, just intensely questioned. No removal of shoes or belts—but they checked your suitcase. Even though it took time, it was efficient and effective. You felt safe when you boarded or exited the plane. I did not live under any false illusions during those years. There were at least two occasions, during my stays in Israel, where just a few minutes made the difference between life and death.

I am pointing this out because after the government introduced TSA into our lives, traveling in and out of America became a living nightmare. A new branch of the U.S. Government became responsible for our National Security which included catching the bad guys in airports—except they forgot that the bad guys were not 99% of Americans. After the Bush and subsequent Obama administrations had gotten rid of profiling, everyone became a suspect. Have you ever seen how they treat elderly American citizens?

I often compared security systems between the two countries and vocally made my observations known when frustrated—not good. Israel profiles. I have seen men and women taken to the side and interrogated before they ever got into the security lines. I have watched questionable characters be pulled out of line or asked to step aside when it was their turn to be questioned. And because Israel profiles, threats are averted quickly and everyday travelers, like myself, are not subject to unnecessary interrogation, search, or seizure.

In Israel, part of profiling is your initial interview with the security team. After being interviewed, you and your luggage are given a number that ranges anywhere from 1-6, six being the highest. If you receive a 6 you are a very high security risk. Israeli security will search all your bags manually and with a high-tech scanning system. And, if available, you will be sent to the body scanner and get your complimentary security massage. The number 6 is not just relegated to suspect terrorists. You may be an American citizen who travels to other Middle Eastern countries, most of which do not have relations with Israel. Or you may make frequent trips to Asia which includes countries like Malaysia and Indonesia. If so, you will receive a higher number and be subject to more stringent security measures; inclusive of character profiling which consists of behavioral and pattern profiling—and Israel's HUMINT (human intelligence) is well trained to recognize all of it.

There is no replacement for profiling. Sadly, profiling has become a racial term—yet, it has little if anything to do with "racism."

So, if not racism what is profiling as it relates to National Security? According to dictionary.com profiling is "the use of personal characteristics or behavior patterns to determine whether a person may be engaged in illegal activity." Does that sound like racism to you?

No, because profiling is not confined to a specific race nor is it singling out a race for vindictive reasons—it is looking for behavior patterns that can potentially lead to danger. In a sense, we are not profiling race; we are profiling evil. We are looking for criminals, drug cartels, fraud rings, smugglers, terrorists, and the like. Unfortunately, many of those categories exist within certain minority communities. Take the Boston Bombers for example—they were of Russian origin and Muslim. In 2011, the FBI was informed by the FSB (Russian Federal Security Service) that Tamerlan, one of the bombers, had become a "radical follower of Islam."[60] In 2012 he traveled to Chechnya and attended a mosque known for its radical ties. Once again, the FBI was warned by the FSB and yet, he returned to America without any security checks. This "turn a blind eye we can't profile" approach by the FBI resulted in three dead Americans and 264 injured innocent civilians.

It is imperative to understand National Security through the looking glass of good and evil, right and wrong, moral and immoral—not race or culture. Terrorism is an evil act committed against people, precious people. So why, was President Obama been so averse to profiling? Could it be because his political interests and affiliations with terrorist organizations had blinded his ability to discern between National Security and the placating of minority and human rights groups? Or did the political makeup of his staff members intervene with our National Security interests?

Regrettably, profiling has become a human rights issue. And the problem often lies with organizations that support human rights activism. These groups twist Constitutional laws to make judges, lawyers, and civilians believe that profiling is a violation of human rights and therefore, racist.

In understanding the challenges that frame the issues surrounding profiling, do you think we should be more involved with profiling? Could profiling improve our National Security? Let's ask President Trump.

୫ଠ

Trump Profile?

On June 19, 2016, Trump told CBS, "Well, I think profiling is something that we're going to have to start thinking about as a country, other countries do it; you look at Israel, and you look at others, and they do it, and they do it successfully. You know, I hate the concept of profiling. But we have to start using common sense."

His speech came after the mass shooting in Orlando, Florida where 49 people were left dead and 40 others injured after a radicalized Muslim opened fire at an LGBT bar. Admittedly, this was not the only terrorist attack on our soil. We have witnessed two on U.S. Army bases, as was the case twice at Ft. Hood. And since the Obama administration did not want to label them as terrorist attacks, the means and methods of deterring them were not utilized.

In a discussion on deterrence of terrorism, Donald Trump referred to the New York Police Department's Demographics Unit that used various means of surveillance on the Muslim communities and Mosques to keep tabs on any uptick of radical behavior. After Bill de Blasio became Mayor, the program was dismantled.

According to the AP-GfK poll conducted March 31 through April 4, 2016, "49% of respondents said that they 'favored surveillance programs aimed at predominantly Muslim communities in the United States to obtain information about possible radicalization.' 47% opposed surveillance." Of course, civil libertarians, Muslims, and others strongly oppose the idea of profiling, arguing that it is unconstitutional and discriminatory based on race, religion, and other factors.[61] New York has had to settle two lawsuits linked to surveillance. And if President Trump and Congress allow a system of profiling to become part of our National Security program, he will face opposition from these communities while attempting to institute its benefits.

Sadly, while updating this book, a terrorist attack struck the heart of New York[62]. Eight lives were snuffed out by an ISIS terrorist, Sayfullo Saipov,[63] just a few blocks away from the World Trade Center Memorial. Why? Firstly, because of the Diversity Visa (No Vetting) Lottery Program initiated by New York's own Senator Chuck Schumer—he traded security for merit. Secondly, no surveillance. According to NJ.com, "The backyard of

Saipov's apartment complex abuts the Masjid Omar Mosque, where many in the community visit each day for prayer services. The mosque was then targeted by NYPD in 2006 in a controversial surveillance program."[64] Sadly, that wasn't the case in 2017.

Trump nailed this issue during his campaign and now, as President, he can bring about the change necessary for the safety of all American citizens—that includes Muslims. Did you know that radical Islam kills its own when they do not adhere to their radical ideology?

80

The Great Wall

Lastly, in our discussion on immigration we must visit the great wall Mexico is going to finance.

Amidst the pro and con Trump sentiments, there was and, among certain media outlets, continues to be a consensus that he is inconsistent and wishy-washy over policy. One of the common rebuttals about Trump is, "he has no consistent policy." If we had a dollar for everyone that told me that, we could pay for the wall!

The truth is that Trump's policies are far more consistent than the media wants to admit. And, to be fair, until he took office, he was an outsider to the Washington web. Meaning that he had to not only follow his gut on what's right and what's wrong with our country, but he also had to learn, along the way, how to develop position statements that were feasible within the context of existing laws and policies. Not an easy task. So, during his campaign I cut him a lot of slack when he addressed issues of great concern to this nation in ways that rubbed people the wrong way.

With that said, many of his position statements, including that of border control and the Wall, are available on his website www.donaldjtrump.com. The position statement we are going to look at now was entitled, "Compelling Mexico to Pay for the Wall."[65] Have you read it? It's good stuff. Let me summarize it for you.

Trump sees our border problem and Mexico's infringement of American sovereignty as a breach of the Patriot Act. The USA Patriot Act was established to "deter and punish terrorist acts in the United States and around the world, to enhance law enforcement investigatory tools, and other purposes." [66] Such deterrence deals with international money laundering, the financing of terrorism, the scrutiny of foreign jurisdiction, foreign financial institutions and classes of international transactions that are subject to criminal abuse. It requires financial services to report potential money laundering and to prevent the use of the U.S. financial system for *personal gain by corrupt foreign officials* and facilitate repatriation of stolen assets to the citizens of countries to whom such assets belong.

Section 326, *Verification of Identification* "prescribes regulations establishing minimum standards for financial institutions and their customers regarding the identity of a client that shall apply to the opening of an account at the financial institution."

In President Trump's words, it is the "know your customer" provision, compelling financial institutions to demand identity documents before opening accounts or conducting financial transactions. Detailed regulations of section 326 are found at 31 CFR 130.120-121.

And because of the Patriot Act section 326 and several other sections, paying for the wall is an easy decision for Mexico. She can make a one-time payment of $5-10 billion to the United States Treasury. In turn, she is ensured that $24 billion in aid continues to flow into her country year after year. What's interesting is how President Trump not only uses the Patriot Act to compel Mexico to finance the wall but how he intends to implement his plan—day by day.

It's too unique not to include in the book:

Day 1: He would promulgate a "proposed rule" to amend 31 CFR 130.121. It would aim to "redefine applicable financial institutions to include money transfer companies like the Western Union and to redefine "account" to include wire transfers. More importantly, it would include a "requirement that no alien may wire money outside of the United States unless the alien first provides a document establishing his lawful presence in the United States."

Day 2: He states that Mexico will protest. It is here that we learn how the $24 billion is remitted to Mexico, via Mexican Nationals working in the United States of which the majority are illegal (well at least 49% as noted in the Pew report).

Day 3: Mexico is told that if they finance the wall, the Trump Administration will not promulgate the final rule and the regulation will not go into effect.

Trump further explained how the use of Trade Tariffs and the enforcement of existing Trade Rules alone will offset losses to U.S. caused by Mexico's unethical subsidy behavior. In turn, providing income gains that will finance the wall. He also talked about "leveraging visas." Canceling visas is an option. Trump said that, "Immigration is a privilege, not a right" and that Mexico is entirely dependent on the United States as a "release valve" for its poverty. We approve hundreds of thousands of visas per year and by adding a small increase to the cost, we would pay for the wall.

The seriousness in which Trump had contemplated the facts and leveraging options regarding Mexico's financing of a system for secure borders reveals more than a controversial plan. It shows us that Trump has American interests at heart, he dislikes inequity and knows the steps necessary to correct the problem. He is intent on securing our borders and has thought through how and why Mexico should aid in paying for the wall. In fact, as of September 2017, eight prototypes were being built across the southern border. Congress funded the prototypes and ultimately, one or two will be chosen for the wall of which President Trump says, "Mexico will be paying ."[67]

Very few leaders are willing to take a politically incorrect stand on issues that are so vital to America's national interests. The scripture speaks about the neighbor who is not equitable. And when he is found out, part of his civic responsibility is to make reparations commensurate up to seven times that which he has unjustly obtained.

The wisdom of Trump's immigration proposals and strategies is restorative while improving our immigration process. Just think, immigrants will no longer have to hide in the shadows of our society. Yes, Trump's immigration views are postured to move us one step closer to making America Great Again.

୫୦

Turning the Tide

In closing, it's important to reiterate that the political divide in our country over foreign immigrants has never been about immigrants per se, but "illegal" immigrants. And all the brouhaha over Trump's Mexican wall has brought some very positive trends to the immigration crisis.

According to Attorney and Professor Allan Wernick (Baruch College), who runs the immigration legal services program at CUNY and writes a twice-weekly immigration column in the Daily News,

> We expect that there's going to be an increased number of people who want to be U.S. citizens. The anti-immigration rhetoric that has driven some candidate's campaigns is leading many immigrants to become citizens, not only so that they can vote, but so that they are protected if the strict policies candidates like Donald Trump have touted are enacted.[68]

> All the bad press is producing something good—legal immigration. Amazing how easy the path to citizenship can be when excuses and unnecessary obstacles are removed.

> Entire volumes can be written about the past, present and future challenges of America's immigration system. I have only touched on a few issues in the forefront because of Trump's nomination and subsequent Presidential victory.

> If you are an immigrant reading this book or a second-generation immigrant, of which I am, or a third or a fourth—the following is what I want you to share with you:

> We love immigrants; this is who we are as a nation: a haven of opportunity and liberty to those escaping

tyranny. And everyone who immigrates to America has a gift, a talent, an idea that they can contribute to building America or making America great again. But those who immigrate must do it legally for three reasons: Immigration gives you significant opportunity, it enables you to work for higher wages, and it keeps you and America safe. Those who come to us from Mexico and South America are escaping communist regimes, ruthless dictators, economic hardship and murderous drug cartels. Those who are refugees from Syria and other Arab nations are fleeing horrific political conditions in which life has no value and destiny has no hope. Surely, you don't want any of the above following you to America! That's why you are leaving![69]

Under President Trump's administration the desire for and commitment to reforming immigration laws can be realized. Such reforms will ensure your legalization and endless opportunity under the banner of the Free while imposing necessary legislation that will make sure that drug cartels, communist insurgents, terrorists and terrorist networks will not find refuge or opportunity in this country! God Bless America and God Bless Our Immigrants

CHAPTER THREE

The House of Lies

"for we have made lies our refuge, and under falsehood have we hid ourselves." Isaiah 28:17

೫

I mmigration is not the only web that was spun and cockatrice egg that was hatched, but it's an important one.

Before we move into other issues that challenge the integrity of Washington D.C. and Trump's Presidency, let's look at the means used to spin the Washington Web: Obama's House of Lies.

Every President has their secrets and not a few have been caught in a lie or two. Take Nixon and his Watergate scandal which is probably no less scandalous than Hillary and her emails or most recently, John Podesta and his emails. Nobody likes to be lied to, but there is a difference between telling a lie or relaying faulty intelligence and being a pathological liar. Remember the saying, "birds of a feather flock together?" Pathological liars beget other pathological liars. And before you know it they have collectively built their entire house on lies.

After taking office in January 2009, President Obama was caught in 1,249 documented cases of lying, lawbreaking, corruption, cronyism, hypocrisy, and waste according to Tim Brown from Freedom Outpost[70] and Daniel Alman, blogger of Dan on Squirrel Hill.[71] That is more than any other or even all Presidents combined.

With this record, no one can say with an honest heart or straight face that our former President didn't have a pathological lying problem. And if we consider that like begets like, Hillary probably clocks in at a close second.

∽

Pathological Liars

What is a pathological liar and how do you spot them?[72] According to Tamara Hill, MS, LPC, whose article was featured in PsychCentral, there are two types of pathological liars, the "compulsive" liar and the "skillful" liar:

> There are Pathological liars who quite frankly cannot help telling so many lies. . ..Their world is much different from our world. But there are also liars who are gratified by telling lies, are good at it, and do not

regret anything they have ever said. These individuals are "skillful" liars who attempt to evade and harm everyone they come across in their lives. In fact, these liars would meet diagnostic criteria for antisocial personality disorder (or sociopathy). They also tell truths in ways that give incorrect perspectives. In other words, they tell the truth in a misleading way to cause people to view things in an incorrect fashion. Such individuals enjoy and get much gratification from keeping you confused and believing their stories. It is the experience of watching a "victim" run through the maze of confusion that gives gratification to most liars.[73]

When I read the above definition, my mind flashed on an incident in our nation's consciousness, the death of Alton Sterling. A young 37-year-old black man who was eulogized as a loving father of five by the Black Lives Matter movement, and whose death was used to incite riots in Louisiana and throughout the country.

Mignon Chambers, Sterling's sister, told WAFB-TV that he was a father of five who had been selling CDs outside the store for years. "I really wanna know more about what happened, about the whole situation, because my brother didn't deserve it. He didn't deserve it at all." Sharida Sterling, his cousin, told The Advocate, "He would have never fought the police, he wouldn't have pulled a gun, he would have been too scared (Facebook)."

Truthfully, no one deserves to die in an unjust manner. And God knows there has been justifiable injustices committed towards the African-American community. But that does not give license to commit falsehood. What Alton's sister and cousin told WAFB-TV was an untruth. A misrepresentation that could be construed as intentionally misleading the public.

The truth is that Alton had a police record for assaulting cops as well as a rap sheet that included rape, gang banging, substance abuse, illegal firearms, failure to pay child support, domestic abuse and the list goes on. To paint this young man as a harmless soul to the public was wrong.

My mother always taught me "if you play with fire, sooner or later you are going to get burned." And unfortunately, Alton's second chances had expired. This was not a white cop hates black boy crime scene. On the contrary, it was about a young man who pushed his luck one too many times.[74][75] Ferguson too—a young man, Michael Brown, who robbed a convenience store and almost took out a cop's eye was portrayed as the victim. The cop, Darren Wilson, was accused of assassinating Michael Brown's character when recounting the events leading up to the incident—i.e. he robbed a convenience store.

What did President Obama have to say about Alton Sterling? Very little; but what he did do was perpetuate a falsehood.

ଈଓ

PsychCentral

Tamara Hill, MS. LPC, writes that there are six telling signs that enable you to recognize when someone is a pathological liar:[76]

1. **Know that a pathological liar will study you**: The goal of the liar may be hidden, but you can count on the fact that they don't want you to know the truth. In order to evade someone, you certainly need to study the person and examine what that person might or might not believe. Liars, often sociopaths, are known to "study" the person they hope to take advantage of. In other words, they look for weaknesses.

2. **Don't forget that the liar lacks empathy**: As hard as it is to believe, it is true. The liar does not have any moral consciousness of how his or her lying behavior may make you feel.

3. **Normal people feel guilty and are relieved when you change the topic or stop asking questions**: A pathological liar is not fazed. You will rarely if ever see emotion.

4. **All liars do not do the common things you think liars do**: Believe it or not, liars do not always touch their nose, shift in their seats or from one foot to the next, or even look sneaky when lying. Some sociopaths have learned how to evade people with

direct eye contact, sociable smiles, and humor. Trust your instincts and discernment. What do their eyes tell you? What does their behavior or laughter tell you?

5. **The most sneaky liars are manipulative:** I once heard someone say, "we all manipulate." While this might be true to a certain degree, the liar tends to manipulate more than anyone else and has learned how to become a "pro" at doing it. There is nothing impressive about the dangerous or evil manipulator.

6. **Pathological liars exhibit strange behaviors:** Some research suggests that pathological liars show no discomfort when caught lying, while other studies suggest that liars may become aggressive and angry when caught. The bottom line is that no pathological liar is the same.

ಐ

1, 249 Lies

If you were to google "Obama's Lies" you would be shocked at the number of articles and lists you would find. From PolitiFact to the Pentagon voices protested the lying that came forth from Obama and his administration. As mentioned above, Dan from Squirrel Hill[77] documented 1,249 well researched lies dating from August 15, 2013, to July 22, 2016. Let's look at a few of these lies.

Lie #1: President Obama had an administration full of lobbyists, after promising he wouldn't have any:

On November 15, 2007, in Las Vegas, Nevada, Obama said that lobbyists " . . . will not work in my White House." However, by February 2010, he had more than 40 lobbyists working in his administration. According to Timothy Carney of the Washington Examiner, Obama had "hired more than 40 ex-lobbyists who now populate top jobs in the Obama administration, including three Cabinet secretaries, the Director of Central Intelligence, and many senior White House officials."[7879]

Of those 40 ex-lobbyists, 10% (4) who were given elite staff positions in the White House and State Department came from the Center for American Progress (CAP), a liberal think tank that has a sister organization Center for American Progress Action Fund (CAP Action). CAP's directors and funders include, none other than, George Soros.[80] Here is the 2009 message from CAP:[81]

> The Center for American Progress—which has emerged as perhaps Washington's most influential idea factory in the age of Obama—is launching a major new war room, to be staffed by nearly a dozen people, that will focus on driving the White House's message and agenda, I'm told. . ..The new war room—which is called Progressive Media—represents a serious ratcheting up of efforts to present a united liberal front in the coming policy wars. The goal of the war room will be to do hard-hitting research that boils down complex policy questions into usable talking

points and narratives that play well in the media and build public support for the White House's policy goals. . ..The war room—a joint project of CAP Action Fund and Media Matters Action Network—will be headed by well-known liberal operative Tara McGuinness who worked on John Kerry's presidential campaign; and during the Bush years was a major player in the anti-war movement.

Lie #2: President Obama had close ties to Wall St., but pretended to support Occupy Wall Street:

Although Obama claimed to support the Occupy Wall St. movement, the truth is that as of 2011, he raised more money from Wall St. than any other candidate during the previous 20 years. In early 2012, Obama held a fundraiser where Wall St. investment bankers and hedge fund managers each paid $35,800 to attend. In October 2011, Obama hired Broderick Johnson, a longtime Wall Street lobbyist, to be his new senior campaign adviser. Johnson had worked as a lobbyist for JP Morgan Chase, Bank of America, Fannie Mae, Comcast, Microsoft, and the oil industry.[82]

Lie #3: President Obama gave tax dollars to AIG executives, then pretended to be outraged about it:

Obama signed a "stimulus" bill that spent money on bonuses for AIG executives. Prior to signing this bill, Obama said, "when I'm president, I will go line by line to make sure that we are not spending money unwisely." However, after reading "line by line" and signing the "stimulus" bill that protected the AIG bonuses, Obama pretended to be shocked and outraged at the bonuses, and said, "Under these circumstances, it's hard to understand how derivative traders at AIG warranted any bonuses at all, much less $165 million in extra pay. . ... How do they justify this outrage to the taxpayers who are keeping the company afloat?" He also said that he would "pursue every single legal avenue to block these bonuses."

Lie #4: President Obama ordered a private company to fire 1,000 employees:

In 2011, after Boeing had hired 1,000 new employees to work at its new factory in South Carolina, the Obama administration ordered Boeing to shut down the factory, because the factory was non-union.

Lie #5: President Obama lied about putting health care negotiations on C-SPAN:

Although Obama had made a campaign promise to have all the health care reform negotiations broadcast on C-SPAN, he broke that promise after being elected. The secrecy of these negotiations was so strong that U.S. Congresswoman and Speaker of the House Nancy Pelosi (D-California) said, "We have to pass the bill so that you can find out what is in it."

Other lies listed on the site include: (173) Hired a retarded man to sell illegal drugs and guns, and then arrested him for doing so; (174) Secretly obtained phone records from Associated Press reporters and editors; (178) Falsely accused a law-abiding news reporter (James Rosen) of being "an aider and abettor and/or co-conspirator" in a criminal investigation; (500) Illegally tried to avoid disclosure of a foreign aid directive that he had signed.[8384]

I have posted the links to Dan's website in the endnotes. It lists the many facets of lies, corruption, and deception that have built Obama's House of Lies. Honestly, it was overwhelming to go through the process of reading them—it just brought tears to my eyes to see so much injustice coming from and around our former Commander-in-Chief.

The problem with lying is that it weaves a web of deception over those who are under it—you might say it casts a spell or brings a curse. Of late, when I listen to sects of Washington perpetuate these same lies it reaffirms how entangled in the Washington Web all associated to the Obama administration became, knowingly or unknowingly, for good or for bad— regardless of reason.

⁊

Does Trump Lie?

Before we move on, let me insert a word about President Trump. There are those who accuse him of lying. So, let's ask the question, "Does Trump lie?"

I really don't know. But most likely the answer would be "yes." Most people do tell a lie here and there and especially, under duress. Have you ever lied when put on the spot? There were statements made throughout his campaign that, when fact checked, were considered false statements or possible lies. With that said, what would make his lying different from that of Barack Obama or Hillary Clinton?

I would like to suggest context and intent. It is highly unlikely, given Trump's track record for opposing Washington corruption and its lies, that he would intentionally lie to mislead the American people. Neither are there any signs that Trump is a pathological liar. On the contrary, most people find him to be too blunt and honest about our problems. And when faced with his own past folly, he fessed up. He didn't weave another lie.

On my university campus, I was asked about Trump by a studious and bright young man from China. He felt very attacked by Trump's accusations toward China's currency manipulation and trade ethics. I told him that in no way was Trump attacking the Chinese people but the ethics of the Government. He then made a statement many of us have said, "I just wish he didn't have to be so forthright about it!" There you have it—that's the reality between Trump's occasional lie and Obama's House of Lies.

ℬ

"If you tell the truth, you don't have to remember anything."

Mark Twain

ℬ

CHAPTER FOUR

American Democracy

"By humility and the fear of the LORD are riches, and honor, and life." Proverbs 22:4

ᔕᏅ

Have you ever thought that maybe, just maybe, the election was not between Hillary Clinton and Donald Trump? Have you ever entertained the possibility that there was more going on behind the scenes than met the eye?

You might be thinking, "of course the election was between Hillary or Trump"—really? Yes, in the eyes of the American public the election appeared to be between these two candidates, but behind the scenes we may find a totally different story. And if so, what story? What could the 2016 national election have been about other than the election of a new President? I would like to suggest that it was about the future direction of our nation and who is going to lead us in that direction. To many, it appeared that the Obama administration was forging the direction of our country; but, as we learned in the first few chapters, there were others—not holding public office—who were shaping the direction of America. And, the leader of the pack was and continues to be George Soros, the man who funded Hillary Clinton's election campaign.

So, as I suggested earlier, could the election have been about two men with two different world views—one man who upholds the Constitution and the foundational principles that made America great, and another man who abhors the Constitution and desperately wants it replaced with a new world order? The order of the borderless, "Open Society?"

From an American perspective, we are already an "open society." We are a bastion of hope to the masses, and a republic that offers its citizens and its immigrants endless opportunity, liberty, and hope. I have lived all over the world and there is no country that can offer its citizens what America does. In America, even the poorest of the poor can find assistance and if desired, run down to the local Starbuck's for a morning coffee.

The American culture is the most heterogeneous and opportunity cultivated culture in the world. Americans love to give, love to help and love to live life to its fullest. Truly, we are made up of every nation, tribe and tongue. And, we love to lead. We have been a role model of freedom, liberty and justice throughout world, that is—until the Obama administration. Even to this day, if I ask an Israeli, "would you like to live in America?" The answer is a passionate, "yes, I would love to live in America." And that holds true with almost every foreigner I meet when I am overseas.

One case and point occurred while discussing visas during a national security class. Out of nowhere a beautiful young lady from Serbia yelled out, "I would love a visa to America."

The following scenario unmasks the depth to which citizens from around the world desire to come to America.

During an eye-opening lecture about the emotions of Egyptian youth during the Arab Spring, we learned how graffiti was used to express their feelings towards government and society. Many young artists painted murals on walls depicting the deep despair, anger and frustration dominating Egyptian society during the Arab Spring uprising.

Unexpectedly, tears started flowing from my eyes as I listened to the question Egyptian youth were asking themselves. In the deepest, darkest night of their nation's struggle for freedom—the younger generation was asking only one question, "where are you America when we need you? You are the one we look to for freedom — where are you?" This was the question that plagued their hearts and minds. They could not understand how a nation that represented freedom, fueled and ignited their desire for change and democracy and then called for the removal of their dictator would leave them to fight alone, to die alone—all in the name of 'American freedom'— shameful!

"Where are you America when we need you? You are the one we look to for freedom — where are you?"

The Arab youth didn't ask, where are you Europe, where are you China, where are you Russia, where are you United Nations, where are you NATO? They asked, "where are you America?"

As I looked over pictures taken of murals calling for help from the streets of Cairo, my heart wept. Silently, I asked myself "where were we?" Only to answer myself, "we were too busy trying not to be America."

If you are an American ask yourself this same question, "where are we?" Is America the same America you grew up in? Is it still the America that champions righteousness and hope to the world? Is it still the Land of opportunity? Will America be there for you, your family, and your neighbor when you need her? Or is there another agenda trying to make America something she's not and you're not?"

ꝏ

America's Honor

Sadly, even though Americans may see America as an "open society" that is not the way George Soros, Barack Obama, Hillary Clinton or European global leaders see America. They see a "closed society"—a society that believes in an old Asiatic tyrant called 'God' and a national declaration which supports that belief: "We hold these truths to be self-evident, that all men are created equal, that they are endowed by their Creator with certain unalienable Rights, that among these are Life, Liberty and the Pursuit of Happiness."

Furthermore, they see the American Constitution as an obstacle to the "open society"— which we discuss later in this chapter. Why? Because it has checks and balances intended to ensure that America never falls into the tyrannical trap of a dictatorship. And, in a more elusive way, they see our Constitution and governmental order as outdated as God Himself. Why? Because, although the idea of democracy can be traced back to the enlightenment period of history, the American Constitution is unique and unlike any other constitution in the world. Our Constitution is based on a distinct biblical pattern of government.[85]

It is very, very important for Americans to understand that America came out of the British commonwealth, a monarchy. A monarchy ruled by a king who, in the eyes of the people, represented God. It is also crucial to understand that the democratic Western world that we refer to as Europe today, was, until the late 1800s and early 1900s, monarchal. On the other hand, America was settled by men and women escaping monarchal tyranny. Religious freedom was the most sought-after liberty from the 1500s forward, and the Bible was the inspiration for our break from England.

The shift in Europe from monarchal to democratic changed more than political powers. For example, when France got rid of its last king during the French Revolution—it also got rid of God. You see, the kings in Europe and the Commonwealth were considered by the people as God's representatives. Hence, *no king equated to no God*—the people rule. To the people, God was the God of the king and the king was a hypocritical tyrant. Therefore, God was viewed as a hypocritical tyrant too.

However, that was not the case of our founding fathers. They believed that the God of Abraham, Isaac, and Jacob was a God of the people—one who watched over them to do them good, not evil. And because this was their perspective two things happened in the forming of the nation we call today, America.

Firstly, as a people we entered into a covenant with God. What nation, apart from ancient Israel has ever entered into a covenant with God? Furthermore, what does that mean exactly? Carole Keller, a prolific writer on American restoration writes,

So, you see, between Europe and the United States there are two distinct democracies. The United States' governing philosophy is based upon the ancient framework of the Ten Commandments. Europe also follows a democratic form of government, but it is not established upon covenantal relations. When comparing America to ancient Israel, the difference is that Israel was a theocracy, and America developed as a Republic, without conscription to a national religion. Thus, America would advance the greatest personal freedom for all people, which would ultimately give America a powerful edge on maintaining peace and order in the world. The promise is unto us, as it was upon Israel in that, if we keep covenant with God, no enemy nation would be able to stand before us. "Every place whereupon the soles of your feet shall tread shall be yours...There shall no man be able to stand before you: for the LORD your God shall lay the fear of you and the dread of you upon all the land that ye shall tread upon, as he hath said unto you."[86]

A covenant is a two-way agreement that is very hard to break. In fact, the covenant between God and Israel cannot be broken. Of this agreement Jeremiah wrote,

Thus saith the LORD, which gives the sun for a light by day, and the ordinances of the moon and of the stars for a light by night, which divides the sea when the waves thereof roar; the LORD of hosts is his name: If those ordinances depart from before me, said the

LORD, then the seed of Israel also shall cease from being a nation before me forever.[87]

Secondly, our government is established by the people and for the people. And, in the case of tyranny, the people have the right to abolish the government and restore it to its covenantal foundations. These foundations began with the Declaration of Independence and were subsequently established by George Washington and the Constitution of the United States of America.

The Declaration of Independence is quite a moving document filled with nuances of revelation. Yet, it distinctly puts center stage the Creator as the chief governing agent of America. And to this ideal the people humbly yoke themselves as is exemplified in the final words of The Declaration of Independence:[88]

We, therefore, the Representatives of the United States of America, in General Congress, Assembled, appealing to the Supreme Judge of the world for the rectitude of our intentions, do, in the Name, and by Authority of the good People of these Colonies, solemnly publish and declare, That these United Colonies are, and of Right ought to be Free and Independent States; that they are Absolved from all Allegiance to the British Crown, and that all political connection between them and the State of Great Britain, is and ought to be totally dissolved; and that as Free and Independent States, they have full Power to levy War, conclude Peace, contract Alliances, establish Commerce, and to do all other Acts and Things which Independent States may of right do. And for the support of this Declaration, with a firm reliance on the protection of divine Providence, we mutually pledge to each other our Lives, our Fortunes and our sacred Honor.

With a signed Declaration and an unratified Constitution, George Washington was nominated as the first President of the United States of America, thirteen years later. He gave the first Presidential oath and the first inaugural address on April 30, 1789. This is the moment when heaven and the United States of America formed an invincible bond. George Washington placed his hand on the bible opened to Genesis chapter 49. He then said, "I do solemnly swear that I will faithfully execute the Office of the President of the United States, and will to the best of my ability, preserve, protect and defend the Constitution of the United States. So, help me God."[89]

Afterwards, he walked into the Senate Chamber and delivered his first inaugural address, opening with a prayer:

It would be peculiarly improper to omit in this first official Act, my fervent supplications to that Almighty Being who rules over the Universe, who presides in the Councils of Nations, and whose providential aids can supply every human defect, that his benediction may consecrate to the liberties and happiness of the People of the United States, a Government instituted by themselves for these essential purposes.

He continues,

No People can be bound to acknowledge and adore the invisible hand, which conducts the Affairs of men more than the People of the United States. Every step, by which they have advanced to the character of an independent nation, seems to have been distinguished by some token of providential agency. . ..Since we ought to be no less persuaded that the propitious smiles of Heaven, can never be expected on a nation that disregards the eternal rules of order and right, which Heaven itself has ordained: And since the preservation of the sacred fire of liberty, and the destiny of the Republican model of Government, are justly considered as deeply, perhaps as finally staked, on the experiment entrusted to the hands of the American people."

♾

A Republican Model

It is here we understand that the forming of the American government was the forming of a Republican model of Government. The anchor of this model was a belief that the Almighty's hand was upon America and His providence would ensure that all her needs were met, and that, overtime, freedoms would be established, prejudices would be abolished, and justice rewarded to citizens of this great country. And upon these two beliefs, imbued within the pages of the Holy Scriptures, was the Constitution and its Bill of rights [90] written and subsequently ratified in December 15, 1791.

Have you ever read the Constitution? It's an amazing document replete with every guiding principle a people would need to be a just, righteous and wise nation.

Of it, Matthew Spalding wrote,

Consider the Constitution. The separation of powers and the system of checks and balances thwarts governmental despotism and promotes responsibility in public representatives. The legitimate constitutional amendment process allows democratic reform at the same time that it elevates the document above the popular passions of the moment, thereby encouraging deliberation and patience in the people. The law inspires caution and encourages mutual checks in our representatives and thereby confines them to their constitutional responsibilities and prevents a spirit of encroachment by government. The people learn from the law-making process to curb their own passions for immediate political change and abide by the legitimate legal process. The demands of good public policy cause the people to be moderate and circumspect.

Good opinions in the people, and good government, have a complementary effect on politics.[91]

Yes, "We the people of the United States, in order to form a more perfect Union, establish Justice, ensure domestic Tranquility, provide for the common Defense, promote the general Welfare, and secure the Blessings of Liberty to ourselves and our Posterity, do ordain and establish this Constitution for the United States of America."

Seriously, though, a Constitution alone cannot govern the hearts of mankind. For that, there needs to be self-government of which George Washington, Thomas Jefferson, James Madison, and Benjamin Frankly all elaborated upon.

James Madison wrote:

[T]he citizens of the United States are responsible for the greatest trust ever confided to a political society. If justice, good faith, honor, gratitude and all the other qualities which ennoble the character of a nation and fulfill the ends of government be the fruits of our establishments, the cause of liberty will acquire a dignity and luster, which it has never yet enjoyed, and an example will be set, which cannot but have the most favorable influence on the rights of Mankind. If on the other side, our government should be unfortunately blotted with the reverse of these cardinal virtues, the great cause which we have engaged to vindicate, will be dishonored and betrayed; the last and fairest experiment in favor of the rights of human nature will be turned against them; and their patrons and friends exposed to be insulted and silenced by the votaries of tyranny and usurpation.

George Washington continued this exhortation in his Farewell Address:

"Religion and morality are indispensable supports. Religion and morality aid good government by teaching men their moral obligations and creating the conditions for decent political life. Thomas Jefferson, the great defender of rights and liberty, put it bluntly when he said that the American people "are inherently independent of all but the moral law."[92]

So, the key components to America's Democracy are: A Republican model of government and the moral law.

⁊

"The American flag is the most recognized symbol of freedom and democracy in the world."

Virginia Foxx

෨

CHAPTER FIVE

European Democracy

"If the foundations be destroyed, what can the righteous do?" Psalm 11:3

℘

O ur Republican model of government was not without its two opposing parties. At the time of the Constitution's conception, there were the Federalists and the Anti-Federalists. Anti-Federalists were those who were in opposition to a strong federal government and the ratification of the Constitution drafted in 1787. In fact, it was not until the Bill of Rights was added to the Constitution that the Anti-Federalists would ratify it. Their preference was for power to remain with states and local governments. On the other hand, the Federalists supported a strong national government and the ratification of the Constitution. They believed that government needed to play a formidable role in managing the debt and tensions following the American Revolution.[93]

The first Federalist party formed by Alexander Hamilton operated from 1792-1824. Other famous Federalists were George Washington and John Adams. Anti-Federalists included Thomas Jefferson, James Monroe, Patrick Henry, Samuel Adams.

Here we get a glimpse into the contention between the two parties over the ratification of the Bill of Rights:[94]

One of the many points of contention between Federalists and Anti-Federalists was the Constitution's lack of a bill of rights that would place specific limits on government power. Federalists argued that the Constitution did not need a Bill of Rights because the people and the states kept any powers not given to the federal government. Anti-Federalists held that a bill of rights was necessary to safeguard individual liberty.

Regardless of the bantering back and forth over the need for government safeguards, there were no qualms about God and the use of His human rights laws as the moral underpinning necessary to sustain this new, and ultimately great, Republic we know as, The United States of America.

This leads us seamlessly into the next series of historical developments that played a role in the development of Europe's democracy. And who leads the way? None other than Thomas Jefferson, the Anti-Federalist.

ℰꙮ

The Right of Man and of the Citizen

In August 1789, under the leadership of Napoleon, the National Constituent Assembly adopted the *Declaration of the Right of Man and of the Citizen*. The significance of its content and origin cannot be underestimated; not only did it become the foundational document of the French Revolution and the basis for the United Nations Universal Declaration of Human Rights adopted in 1948, but it also had a direct impact on liberty and democracy throughout all of Europe and the world.[95]

Its origins, though, in principle are biblical and distinctly American. Inspired by the American Revolution as well as the Enlightenment principles of human rights, General Lafayette worked closely with Thomas Jefferson, the principal architect of the Declaration of Independence. It is not a coincidence that Thomas Jefferson was in France as a U.S. diplomat when the French Declaration was constructed. Jefferson was able to draw from numerous foundational documents that formed the ideal of America including The Virginia Declaration of Rights and The U.S. Bill of Rights.[96] His influence is clearly seen in the very first line of the French Declaration: "Article I - Men are born and remain free and equal in rights. Social distinctions can be founded only on the common good."

The Declaration also ushered in the end of feudalism by asserting popular sovereignty over the divine right of kings—a principle expressed by Benjamin Franklin, "In free governments, the rulers are the servants and the people their superiors and sovereigns."[97] Thus favored treatment of nobility and clergy was eliminated as stated, "All the citizens, being equal in the eyes of the law, are equally admissible to all public dignities, places, and employments, according to their capacity and without distinction other than that of their virtues and their talents."[98] It was the beginning of the end of the Holy Roman Empire and monarchal Europe, as they knew it.

What is absent in the *Declaration of the Right of Man and of the Citizen* and its subsequent offspring, the *United Nations Declaration of Human Rights* is the mention of God as the source of human rights. This is, of course, the telltale sign of Frances's and ultimately Europe's rejection of God along with its removal of kings. The other aspect absent in these two declarations is, "moral law."

From the time of the French Revolution up until World War II, there were numerous developments that changed the landscape of monarchial Europe. One such development took place in Germany with the establishment of the Weimar Republic—Germany's first democratic form of Government. Sadly, it was short-lived due to the rise of Christian Nationalism and the ideology of the State. The ideology of the state is crucial to understanding "where God went" when he was removed alongside monarchal rule.

It was Georg Hegel, [99] a renowned Protestant theologian, and a German philosopher, who, in his assessment of power and ownership of the rights of man, transferred all from the religious institutions to the State:

> The Universal is to be found in the State. . ..The State is the Divine Idea as it exists on earth. . ..We must, therefore, worship the State as the manifestation of the Divine on earth. . ..The State is the march of God through the world.[100]

Karl Popper noted that Hegel's view was "absolute moral authority of the State, which overrules all personal morality, all conscience."[101] And of the bearer of the Ten Commandments and its enigma Christianity Martin Bormann, head of the Parteikanzlei (Nazi Party Chancellery) and Hitler's private secretary publicly stated:

> National Socialist and Christian concepts are incompatible, . ..Our National Socialist worldview stands on a much higher level than the concepts of Christianity, which in their essentials were taken over from Judaism. For this reason, too, we can do without Christianity.[102]

So, let's recap that last few statements. First, we see that moral authority has shifted from God and self-government to the State as a Divine idea to be worshiped.

Just as the king was looked upon as the one who ruled in God's stead, now the State is seen as the authority that rules in God's stead—real progress eh? The scary part is what follows. Now, the State is the moral conscience of men. There is no need for self-government or an individual to think on his own, the State does it for you! It is your conscience! What does that mean? It can develop your values and moral compass, apart from God. This led to the State no longer needing Christianity or Judaism for guidance, because the National Socialist worldview reached a much higher plane. Let me ask you, do you think you can get much higher than the Almighty Himself?

And if you think that's frightening, hold onto your jaw because it's about to drop.

෨

God is Dead

Nothing underscores these developments in Europe more than Fredrick Nietzsche and his famous observation: "God is dead, and the church killed him."[103] Now, if society wants to get rid of God how do they do it? Even though the king was removed, there was still the moral code rooted in the Ten Commandments present in the citizens of Christian Europe. So, the next logical step was to remove it. And that was precisely what the Nazi party and Hitler set out to do.

Of the Ten Commandments Hitler said,

The day will come when I shall hold up against these commandments the tables of a new law. And history will recognize our movement as the great battle for humanity's liberation, a liberation from the curse of Mount Sinai, from the dark stammering's of nomads who could no more trust their own sound instincts, who could understand the divine only in the form of a tyrant who orders one to do the very things one doesn't like. This is what we are fighting against: the masochistic spirit of self-torment, the curse of so-called morals, idolized to protect the weak from the strong in the face of the immortal law of battle, the great law of divine nature. Against these so-called Ten Commandments, against them we are fighting.[104]

Yes, you read it correctly. Hitler blamed the ills of the world on the Ten Commandments or as he said, "the curse of so-called morals." So, let's look at these morals and ask ourselves "what exactly are the Ten Commandments if not the bedrock of true human rights?"

To the Founding Fathers of America, the Ten Commandments are the very foundation of what men call the "issues of life." They are the plumb line of right and wrong, good and evil, holy and profane within the conscience of mankind. They were and continue to be the Divine moral code that Herbert Huffmon, an expert in Old Testament studies, says "concern matters of fundamental importance in both Judaism and Christianity." He writes,

They reveal the greatest obligation of mankind—to worship only God. They underscore the value of human life and the greatest injury to a person— murder. They highlight the covenant of marriage and reveal the greatest injury to family bonds—adultery. The teach men ethics in business while emphasizing that the greatest injury to commerce and law is fraud and lying—bearing false witness. They instruct children on the greatest inter-generational obligation— honor to parents. They show us that the greatest obligation to a community is truthfulness and that the greatest injury to your neighbor and his moveable property is theft.[105]

In his writings to the Romans, Paul mentions five of the Ten Commandments and their association with neighborly love:

Owe no man anything, but to love one another: for he that loves another has fulfilled the law. For this, you shall not commit adultery, you shall not kill, you shall not steal, you shall not bear false witness, you shall not covet; and if there be any other commandment, it is briefly comprehended in this saying, namely, you shall love thy neighbor as thyself. Love works no ill to his neighbor: therefore, love is the fulfilling of the law.[106]

Sadly, the very Commandments that were to bring life, liberty and the pursuit of happiness to the nation of Israel and any country who would adopt them, became the yoke that every generation has struggled with and that which governments have attempted to unburden themselves from.

We learn from Hermann Rauschning,[107] well known for his book *Voice of Destruction*, and other eyewitness accounts of Hitler's ranting that, "Hitler and his malleable henchmen hated God's law. They knew that it was the only thing that stood between them and their new world order. And that the God of the Bible as described by Hitler was "that Asiatic tyrant." Also, real freedom was freedom from God's law."[108] I might add, that by hating God's laws they innately hated the Jews—for they were and are the bearers of God's covenants and His laws.

This brings us to the two points of separation between the two democracies: God and His Moral Law.

ᴤꙩ

Church and State

Now you may be reading this and wholeheartedly believe in the separation of Church and State. And you should. The last thing you want is the Church running the State or the Federal government. Can you imagine that? Scary, right? Just figuring out which Church would rule would require how many committees? No thanks!

On the other hand, a strong, stable government is rooted in a foundational faith.

For example, China is a communist country that boasts three religions: Confucianism, Taoism, and Buddhism. The official position of the Chinese Communist Party-State government is a Marxist-Leninist-Maoist atheism which believes that religion will die out as social conditions evolve. Even though this is the official position of the government and its members must support such, the reality is that the government is funding a revival of Confucianism and over 20% of its society practices Buddhism. The Chinese government's motive for supporting Confucianism is to counter Western influence and replace it with anti-Western and anti-modern nationalism. Also, on the fringe, the government allows for forms of state-controlled Protestantism and Chinese Catholicism.

With that said, an anti-Western agenda does not mean anti-moral or anti-value sentiment. On the contrary, Asian culture holds the family unit and social values central to its society. Hence, they see Western society as morally bankrupt—anything goes in the name of tolerance under the banner of the name of Human Rights. This is a threat to their societal core. Amidst all its religious diversity from atheism to Buddhism, Confucianism to state controlled Christian institutions, there is a moral framework woven in their religious base. Also, there is an emerging ethos of biblical ethics. This is likely due to the shifting religious landscape of China towards Judeo-Christianity. This is confirmed by a burgeoning underground Pentecostal Christian movement estimated at around 35 million [109] and a growing Israeli-Jewish presence in cities like Shanghai.[110]

How ironic would it be if China becomes a Judeo-Christian nation and America wastes away into nihilism? Not possible? It's already happening. One of the largest movements in China is the back to Jerusalem movement. A Christian based organization that believes China plays a huge role in the restoration of Israel and the return of the Messiah. Fifteen years ago, when I lived in Asia, I was teaching Hebrew to the Chinese. In one of my classes I had over 55 Chinese students, can you imagine? And today, while living in Israel, I am constantly interacting with Chinese students, businessmen, and women. And of those who profess Buddhism our conversations always veer in the direction of Judaism and Christianity—wild, eh?

India is another rising superstar. Its national religion maybe Hinduism which is reflected in its cultural practice, but its Constitution is structured after the U.S. Constitution. And, although, much of India's leadership is part of the elite ruling caste system, its moral underpinnings hold a close association to the Torah.[111] Once again, we see a shift towards the acceptance of the Judeo-Christian belief system. India is also becoming a close friend and ally of Israel.

Russia, as well as African countries like Nigeria, are good examples of strong governments that have incorporated a semblance of a biblical moral framework into the foundational underpinnings of their society. By no means is the Russian government even remotely accepting of biblical faith, apart from its national pseudo-religion encapsulated in the Russian Orthodox Church. But, as a Marxist communist government, it repeatedly shunned former President Obama's push towards a more liberal human rights platform that abandon's God's Human Rights laws. Nigeria too objected to Obama's call for a more progressive platform of human rights that was in direct conflict with Nigeria's collective conscience and God's Human Rights laws. Nigeria considers itself a Christian nation currently in a life and death battle against radical Islam—another faith system that holds an appearance of God's Human Rights laws without the key components such as justice and mercy.

So, to recap, we are seeing countries that hold dear to their foundational moral and cultural ethics emerging on the global stage. While a Western culture that is throwing off its moral constraints in the name of "Human Rights," is in deep, deep, trouble.

And America? As we continue to desensitize ourselves to our moral conscience and our foundational history, we spiral further and further into civil and political anarchy. Consider that our nation is embroiled in violent racial debates inclusive of unprecedented murders of citizens and law enforcement, indoctrination of youth that fosters acts of mass killings in our schools, and liberal, throw your conscience out the window, politics that created a cesspool of iniquity in government. The gaping hole of moral and spiritual decline within American society is being filled with drug cartels, terrorist cells, illegal immigration, anti-American and anti-God ideologies, increasing rates of suicide, a staggering national debt and a lascivious society that has very little self-control. Wow, that's a mouthful—is it really that bad? I hope not.

On that note, I think it is time to reconsider, not the role of the Church in governmental affairs, but the role of God's Human Rights Laws along with the biblical precepts that undergirded our government and made America great in the first place. These are the Laws that George Washington, Thomas Jefferson, and James Madison spoke of and adopted. The principals that enabled our nation to come out from under European tyranny and rise to lead the Free World. It is God's Human Rights laws and their instruction that will bring about the social justice our nation is desperately crying for.

଼

Post WWII: 1968

Immediately following WWII, the nations gathered to adopt a solution to the atrocities of the war. Their solution? *The United Nations Universal Declaration of*

Human Rights. For the most part, this declaration remained in limbo throughout the Cold War; the counter culture of the 1960s and the year 1968[112] being the exception.

1968 was a year of unprecedented civil unrest in America and around the world. It was the end of America's leadership in the Vietnam War. I want to deviate for a second to ensure our readers understand the Vietnam War and America's role in this war. To accomplish this, the following assertion provides an excellent summary taken from HistoryNet[113]:

> The Vietnam War is the commonly used name for the Second Indochina War, 1954–1973. It refers to the period when the United States and other members of the SEATO (Southeast Asia Treaty Organization) joined the forces of the Republic of South Vietnam to contesting the communist Viet Cong (VC), and the North Vietnamese Army (NVA). The U.S. had the largest foreign military presence and directed the war from 1965 to 1968. For this reason, in Vietnam today it is known as the American War. It was a direct result of the First Indochina War (1946–1954) between France, which claimed Vietnam as a colony, and the communist forces then known as Viet Minh. In 1973, a "third" Vietnam war was a continuation, actually between North and South Vietnam, but without significant U.S. involvement. It ended with a communist victory in April 1975.

The Vietnam War was the longest in U.S. history, until the war in Afghanistan that began in 2002 and continues at this writing (2013). It was incredibly divisive in the U.S., Europe, Australia and elsewhere. Because the U.S. failed to achieve a military victory and the Republic of South Vietnam was ultimately taken over by North Vietnam, the Vietnam experience became known as "the only war America ever lost." It remains a very controversial topic that continues to affect political and military decisions today.

The Vietnam War and more specifically the TET offensive[114] awakened the American public to the reality of war.[115] What I mean by this is, that, before the Vietnam war, the American people were not subject to the blood, guts, and horrors of war in "real time." Radio and movie theaters updated us on the details during previous wars and, it did so in a way that did not expose the American public to the gorier side of war. Of course, film and photography shocked the American and world conscience when it exposed WWII's unimaginable horrors of the death camps and the slaughter of six million Jews—but its disclosure was not in "real time."

The Vietnam War and the TET offensive were televised. When the American people saw the shooting of innocent Vietnamese and the burning of their homes, they no longer could condone such a War. The "real time" exposure violated the American collective conscience causing the younger generations to take the streets.

Protests and civil unrest turned the war into a political nightmare manifest in the abandonment of honor and respect towards of military. Such reproach of our soldiers was undeserving, but the collective conscience of our nation was wounded, and it reflected such in its disdain towards government and those obeying their commands.

In addition to the War, the civil rights movement was continuing to make great strides in equality. Sadly, both Martin Luther King, Jr. and Robert Kennedy were murdered. The reason for Kennedy's death is interesting: On June 5th, 1968 at 12:13 AM, Kennedy was shot by Sirhan Sirhan, a 24-year-old Jordanian. The motive for the shooting was apparent anger over several pro-Israeli speeches Kennedy had made during his campaign.[116]

May 1968 marked the Parisian student revolt in France that escalated until, on May 22, there were over nine million workers on strike. In October, there was a similar student uprising in Mexico City. It seems like everyone who had a gripe revolted. Even the Women's Liberation groups, joined by members of New York NOW, demonstrated at the Miss America Beauty Contest in Atlantic City calling for the dismissal of traditional feminine roles and the symbolic burning of the bra.

In August, Russia crushed the Prague Spring in Czechoslovakia and Chicago became a battery zone between anti-war demonstrators and the police during the Democratic National Convention. And then there was "Mark Rudd, a college junior who returned from a trip to

Cuba, 'fired up with the flame of socialist revolution' to help direct a massive anti-war sit-in at Columbia University. Also, at the time, many high school and college students smoked grass, dropped acid and listened to the Beatles, Janis Joplin and Jimi Hendrix."[117]

Other events included the birth of Intel, the launch into Orbit of Apollo 7 and Apollo 8, the election of Nixon, and the halt of U.S. bombings in Vietnam.

Jack Torry, who wrote a phenomenal overview of 1968 in his 2008 article, *Chaotic 1968 changed America forever,* ended it with the words of Mark Kurlansky:[118]

America's most turbulent year since the Civil War ended in "an instant when racism, poverty, the wars in Vietnam and the Middle East" were "shoved aside" by the dramatic flight of Apollo 8, Mark Kurlansky wrote in his book, 1968: The Year that Rocked the World. On the evening of Dec. 24, as Apollo 8 carried humans around the moon for the first time, astronauts William Anders, Jim Lovell and Frank Borman broadcast to the world vivid images of Earth and read from the book of Genesis. As he finished, Borman added, "And from the crew of Apollo 8, we close with good night, good luck, a Merry Christmas, and God bless all of you—all of you on the good Earth."

1968 was what many would call "America's Coming of Age" the end of ten years of "mindless violence," and even, the "end of American Idealism." In retrospect, it was also a year of change that brought the American government to face issues that were festering under the surface of our society. Undoubtedly, it revealed the breaking down of our moral framework, but even more so, a coming to terms with a flawed criminal and social justice system that had failed the people. One that, the American people would have to face again.

଼

After the Cold War

It could be said of the Cold War that it was a "blessing in disguise." Following WWII, Europe was in shambles physically, psychologically, ideologically and spiritually. The Cold War between America and Russia gave Europe time to come to terms with the horrors of the war and rebuild. Following the election of Ronald Reagan miraculous events began to happen in world affairs. No longer could the U.S. and Russia remain in a headlock and Germany remain divided. It took a leader with moral character to stand at the Brandenburg Gate in West Berlin, Germany on June 12, 1987, and say:

Mr. Gorbachev, Mr. Gorbachev, "Tear down this wall."

What did the wall represent? Separation, division, a stranglehold on hope for all people. What did its collapse represent? Society's cry for no more walls! No more borders!

Let's now move into the next chapter and discuss the ideological and current political developments surrounding our two democracies—especially borders.

ℰℴ

"When you move a border, suddenly life changes violently. I write about nationality."

Alan Furst

ဆာ

CHAPTER SIX:

It's All About Borders

"Thou has set all the borders of the earth: . . ."
Psalm 74:17

ℰↄ

H ow would one sum up the world-views of George Soros and Donald Trump in a few words? "A man without borders" and "A man with borders."

Borders are a unique phenomenon in the earth. Of them, Asaph wrote in Psalm 74:17, "Thou has set all the borders of the earth: thou has made summer and winter." The Hebrew word for borders is גבולה (gebulah) and it means, "a boundary, region: —a border or territory." Figuratively, it also can refer to "a region or territory of darkness." The first mention of the word "border" is in Genesis 10:19; where we read about "the border of the Canaanites." It occurs 241 times in the Hebrew scriptures, and its last mention is in Malachi 1:5, "And your eyes shall see, and you shall say, The LORD will be magnified from the border of Israel."

Often, conflicts and wars begin with the coveting of another nation's borders. Germany's doctrine of Lebensraum, expansion to provide "living space" for its citizens, started two World Wars. Furthermore, before the 20th century, the historical geopolitical landscape was fraught with imperial expansion from the ancient Akkadian empire whose territory was that of today's Iraq (2,350-2,150 BCE), until the 20th-century collapse of the Ottoman and British empires. Since, the fall of these last two empires and the rise of national Israel there has not been a modern day empirical expansion—or has there?

After Europe had time to think about what happened during WWII there was a post-Cold War push for a non-violent, no war Europe. As one who has extensively studied European and Holocaust history, I think the one who lost out in WWII and post-modern Europe was God. Not only did He lose over six million of his children and any repository for the Judeo-Christian faith (meaning that the institution of Judeo-Christianity collapsed after WWII), but He also lost all moral footing in Europe. Wasn't that exactly what Hitler wanted—A world without God's moral code known as the Ten Commandments? Let's revisit Hitler's words:

The day will come when I shall hold up against these commandments the tables of a new law. And history will recognize our movement as the great battle for humanity's liberation, a liberation from the curse of Mount Sinai, from the dark stammering's of nomads who could no more trust their own sound instincts, who could understand the divine only in the form of a tyrant who orders one to do the very things one doesn't like. This is what we are fighting against the masochistic spirit of self-torment, the curse of so-called morals, idolized to protect the weak from the strong in the face of the immortal law of battle, the great law of divine nature. Against these so-called Ten Commandments, against them, we are fighting.[119]

Removing God's Human Right's Laws from society and categorizing them as "the curse of so-called morals," as if they were to blame for all of Europe's ills, was the first and most formidable boundary to be removed. Think about the value of just one of the Ten Commandments: "Thou shall not murder." How valuable is this law to the peace, safety, and national security of a nation? Would there have been a Holocaust if this law was upheld?

The second phase of removing boundaries came with the rise of the European Union and the vision of an "open society" in the form of a borderless Europe.

Of the European Union George Soros said:

"The European Union was a very inspiring idea to people like me." Reflecting back to when European economies were more balanced, "It was the embodiment of the idea of an open society, like-minded countries getting together and sacrificing part of their sovereignty for the common good. It was meant to be a voluntary association of equals."[120]

The European Union's initial move in creating an "open society" was first to remove the national sovereignty of nation states. This was part of a post-war doctrine that believed "borders are the source of war." This belief system drives the view of George Soros, the European Union and, as we will see, the United Nations. The "open society" utopian goal is: one world, one government, one rule of law. In other words, one big happy family—no more war. Unfortunately, this worldview has created a vacuum of evil, and we are only beginning to watch the horrors of it.

℃

Uh Oh NGO's

The European Union is not the only borderless institution George Soros is supporting. There are also non-government organizations known as NGO's. These organizations are not subject to the sovereign boundaries of nations, but they are subject to other entities like the Open Society Foundation (OSF). Leaked Soros emails revealed that OSF funded at least 75 NGO's to manipulate the European elections. This network came under the umbrella of the Open Society Initiative for Europe (OSIFE). That's just Europe. According to the NGO Monitor, Soros also funds numerous anti-Israel and Palestinian political advocacy NGO's. Here is a sample list:

Adalah (amount unknown), Al-Haq (amount unknown), Al Mezan (amount unknown) Breaking the Silence (NIS330,990 in 2015), B'Tselem (amount unknown), Center for Constitutional Rights ($495,000 in 2015), Mada al Carmel (amount unknown), American Friends Service Committee (amount unknown), Palestinian Center for Human Rights (amount unknown), Mossawa (amount unknown).

The NGO Monitor update on Soros released this statement as well: On August 14, 2016, leaked documents from OSF were posted anonymously on the DC Leaks website. A number of these unverified documents deal with OSF's grants to political NGOs through its "Arab Regional Office (ARO)—Palestinian Citizens of Israel" department. Headed by Ammar Abu Zayyad, the ARO is one of several funding mechanisms for Israeli and Palestinian NGO's in the OSF network.

And what about the United States? How many NGO's has Soros funded to manipulate the U.S. elections? Well, the philanthropy of Soros supports over 150 U.S. based NGO's, several of which most Americans are familiar.

One I would like to highlight regarding the election is the Center for American Progress: "This leftist think tank is headed by former Clinton chief of staff John Podesta, works closely with Hillary Clinton, and employs numerous former Clinton administration staffers. It is committed to 'developing a long-term vision of a progressive America' and 'providing a forum to generate new progressive ideas and policy proposals.'"

What is mind boggling to me is how a Jewish Holocaust survivor can continue to foster the underlying ideology of Hitler, knowingly or unknowingly through his far-reaching support of NGO's that promote flagrant demonizing anti-Israel agendas.

Before we move on to discuss non-state actors, the following is the DCLeaks website summary of their findings surrounding George Soros:

George Soros is a Hungarian-American business magnate, investor, philanthropist, political activist and author who is of Hungarian-Jewish ancestry and holds dual citizenship. He drives more than 50 global and regional programs and foundations. Soros is named as the architect and sponsor of almost every revolution and coup around the world for the last 25 years. The USA is thought to be a vampire due to him and his puppets, not a lighthouse of freedom and democracy. His minions spill blood of millions and millions of people just to make him even more rich. Soros is an oligarch sponsoring the Democratic party, Hillary Clinton, hundreds of politicians all over the world. This website is designed to let everyone inside of George Soros' Open Society Foundation and related organizations. We present you the work plans, strategies, priorities and other activities of Soros. These documents shed light on one of the most influential network operating worldwide.

ഇ

Non-State Actors

In addition to the European Union and the NGO's, you have the Palestinians who are non-state actors. Non-state actors (NSA) are "entities that participate or act in international relations. They are organizations with sufficient power to influence and cause a change even though they do not belong to any established institution of a state." Terrorist organizations like Hamas, Al Qaeda, Hezbollah, and ISIL are considered "violent non-state actors." The Open Society Foundation has created a propaganda narrative to make the Palestinians appear to the world as if they are a legitimate country with borders being victimized by a non-legitimate country, Israel—how perverted is that? What's even more disturbing is, this non-state actor has influence over international law as well as voting and veto powers in the both the European Union and the United Nations.

And then there is ISIL whose vision is to take over the world. It is trying to create a Caliphate (a territory ruled by a Caliph) by removing national borders in the Middle East and setting up territory governed by Sharia Law.

All of the above-mentioned State and non-state actors inclusive of institutions, NGO's, and terrorist organizations, play a direct or indirect role in Soros' worldview. With his billions of dollars, he promotes democratic liberalism and a world without borders— his "Open Society."

About today's European Union, Soros says, "I want to preserve the EU as a whole. That's a job that isn't going to be completed in my lifetime. I want the wealth that I have built up to last and to not be lost, so the foundations I have started will go on after I die."[121]

In the world of George Soros borders or boundaries, moral or legal, indicate a "closed society" and need to be removed. Interestingly, this idea of "removing borders" is not unique. Isaiah wrote about this scary scenario 2,500 years ago:

> By the strength of my hand I have done it, and by my wisdom; for I am prudent: I have removed the boundaries of the people, and have robbed their treasures, and I have put down the inhabitants like a valiant man: And my hand has found as a nest the riches of the people: and as one gathers eggs that are left, have I gathered all the earth: and there was none

that moved the wing, or opened the mouth, or peeped.[122]

The individual described in the above passage was the king of Assyria. Although the king of Assyria was a real king, this passage also possesses a figurative understanding that likens the king of Assyria to evil leaders, to Satan, or any enemy of God who removes the bounds of the people.

The ancient Assyrian Empire spanned four modern day countries: Syria, Iraq, Turkey and Iran. While Israel was under the reign of King Hezekiah, the king of Assyria threatened to destroy the cities of Judah. To appease the king, Hezekiah made a secret side deal for all the gold and silver in the treasury of the House of the LORD. Hezekiah even stripped the gold from the doors of the Temple— probably just shy of the 1.3 billion and 400 million the U.S. government has given Iran. And if Hezekiah's secret appeasement of Assyria wasn't bad enough, it gets worse. During the time of Hezekiah's illness, he received precious gifts from the king of Babylon (modern day Iraq). So, after he received divine healing of his terminal illness he returned the kindness by inviting the king of Babylon to Jerusalem—so what's wrong with that? Well, upon the arrival of the king and his delegation, Hezekiah gave them a personal tour of the kingdom's treasury—top secret stuff, and he showed them everything.

It is like inviting the Chinese, the Russians (uh oh weren't 13 indicted in 2018?), and the Muslim Brotherhood into the White House, Pentagon, and Treasury, and then scratching your head wondering how and why they are hacking your government encrypted military systems and stealing your top military secrets. How could Hillary even remotely be surprised of her computer hack after allegedly sharing top secret information with our enemies? And you wonder why we have serious national security concerns?

The story of Assyria removing the boundaries of surrounding nations and its analogies pale in comparison to how the Nazi Regime removed the bounds of the Jews during WWII. It began with benches, then restaurants, then businesses, then homes and then wealth. They were moved from communities into ghettos, from ghettos into camps, and from camps into ovens—and the whole world was silent, nobody peeped.

When we think of a borderless Open Society, we cannot ignore BREXIT. Boundaries were a central issue driving Britain's referendum and the Leave campaign. As part of the European Union, Britain had all but lost its ability to control its borders. Hence, as a nation, they were not only subject to increased terrorism, but also to the economic chaos created by the Syrian Refugee crisis and other migration issues. Furthermore, Britain suffered a massive loss in their fishing industry due to the redistribution of water rights to Sweden. And when they woke up from the mirage of an Open Society, they saw the danger of placing their borders into the hands of E.U.

Israel too fell prey to the illusion of the Open Society doctrine. In 2005, Israel succumbed to International and American pressure and relinquished its southern territory of the Gaza strip known as, Gush Katif. This piece of land was handed over to the Palestinians as is, with all their homes and thriving businesses. This handover was completed despite repeated warnings that the territory would be taken over by Hamas and used as a military and terrorist training base. Even though Israelis voted against it, the Prime Minister moved forward due to American pressure—the results were as warned. A choice that has cost Israel dearly. Since 2005, Israel's non-aggression position has been used by the Palestinians to incite violence and paint an international image of Israel as the aggressor and oppressor. Again, this narrative is a falsehood of inordinate proportions—it is Hamas that is the aggressor and the PLO who is the oppressor of the Palestinian people.

Let me ask you, as a homeowner, "Do you have boundaries and land rights? How willing are you to share your front or backyard with your neighbors?" You might love them, but if they camped on your side of the fence, would you just join them sitting around the campfire singing Kumbaya? Of course, not! So, why would anyone agree to an Open Society ideology by letting a government remove borders? And, I don't say this only of

Europe. Prior to Trump taking office, Obama had "Open Society" fever. Remember how he wanted to disband U.S. borders with his two amigos Canada and Mexico? Do you see how Trump's election halted the progress of Soros' Open Society agenda?

Let's now look at the origin of this Open Society doctrine.

℘

Karl Popper

Who shaped the worldview of George Soros? In many ways, it originates from his mentor and professor, Karl Popper.

Karl Popper was a famous philosopher of science. Both his grandparents were Jewish. After his family moved to Vienna, they converted to Lutheranism for the sole purpose of climbing the social ladder. Popper, who was a professing Lutheran in his younger years ended up an agnostic, of which he said, "I don't know whether God exists or not. Some forms of atheism are arrogant and ignorant and should be rejected, but agnosticism—to admit that we don't know and to search—is all right."[123] He notably feared God, at some level, because in a 1969 interview he said, "When I look at what I call the gift of life, I feel gratitude which is in tune with some religious ideas of God. However, the moment I even speak of it, I am embarrassed that I may do something wrong to God in talking about God."[124]

Although he objected to organized religion and the fascism it birthed in Europe, at the heart of his argument was his struggle with the reality that God could be partial to a "particular group" of people—the Jews—known as "the chosen people." Here is a summation of his thoughts:

> He objected to organized religion, saying, "it tends to use the name of God in vain." He noted that there was a danger of fanaticism because of religious conflicts: "The whole thing goes back to myths which, though they may have a kernel of truth, are untrue. Why then should the Jewish myth be true and the Indian and Egyptian myths not be true?" In a letter, he stressed his tolerant attitude: "Although I am not for religion, I do think that we should show respect for anybody who believes honestly."[125]

To solve the problem of the differences in race, social classes, and religious faiths, Karl Popper developed an argument and narrative for "democratic liberalism" known today as the "doctrine of tolerance." He spoke of two types of societies: the "closed society" and the "open society." Within his book, *The Open Society and Its Enemies* we get a glimpse into exactly who are those *closed societies.*

Closed societies are societies or organizations that base their existence on what Popper calls, "Historicism." These can include Marxists who "do not wish to relieve men from the strain of their responsibilities" or "the Chosen

People—the Jews" or "any national society whose foundational belief system and moral code includes God and the Ten Commandments."

Open Societies, on the other hand, are organizations like the European Union. Societies which engage in the blurring of borders, races, cultures, sovereignty, or shared societal values and norms. Societies which "tolerate everybody" even the *terrorists* who are bombing the crap out of their countries.

Take, for example, former President Obama's global push for "homosexual marriage rights." To his dismay, some nations believe that marriage is still between one man and one woman and that homosexual marriage is an aberration of such. Now, according to individuals like Karl Popper, Barack Obama, and George Soros, those nations are "closed societies" because they have a societal moral code and belief system that sees homosexuality as a moral issue, not a matter of human rights. In an *Open Society*, moral standards cannot be imposed upon its citizens because they produce intolerance. So, in place of ethical and moral relevancy in steps, Human Rights.

℘

Alan Dershowitz

Of "human rights" famed International Human Rights lawyer, Alan Dershowitz said on ILTV's weekly program *One on One with Alan Dershowitz*:

The greatest tragedies that have occurred in the last twenty years is the hijacking of the human rights agenda—turning human rights into human wrongs. Using human rights, not as a shield to protect vulnerable people, but as a sword directed only against Israel. And, the real victims of this have been the victims of genocide around the world, because they don't get the attention they ought to get–because the attention of the International Community is focused almost exclusively on Israel.

Dershowitz's observation of "human rights" leads us back to the Open Society. According to Soros the Open Society is:

A condition where individuals with equal access to knowledge generate the wisdom to create a humane society and laws to maintain political freedoms and human rights. In contrast, "closed societies" such as dictatorships, restrict knowledge and enforce conformity through possession of what they claim are universal truths, and then by legal and cultural means.[126]

After reading Soros' expose´ of a "closed society" you would think he is referring to countries like Venezuela, Cuba, Saudi Arabia, Syria, Kuwait, Libya, Tunisia, and the like, wouldn't you? What if I told you he is speaking about America and Israel? That would be crazy, right?

If you follow the organizations funded by Soros and his Open Society Foundation, you would quickly learn what he deems as a "closed society"—a society that holds any belief system and trust in the God of Abraham, Isaac, and Jacob. This holds true for both America and Israel. Both nations uphold the tenets of scripture as the framework of their democracy—the rights of all men to liberty, justice and the pursuit of happiness.

What's the alternative to the Soros' "closed society"? An Open Society with Human Rights as its religion. In America, we experienced Open Society ideology throughout Obama's administration, especially during his second term. Let's see how well that worked. Did it produce a more tolerant society? A happier and more prosperous society? A more equitable society? What about a more peace loving and righteous society? Or did it produce overreaching government, corrupt lobbyists, and politicians paid to destroy societal norms and further entitled citizenship? And what about society's view towards conservatism and our Judeo-Christian faith–better or worse?

What type of tolerance did it produce? Well, if you think of men like Al Sharpton, Rev. Wright, and Louis Farrakhan as tolerant—then we did well. How about a more equitable society? Equitable *does not* mean, "equal rights"; it means, "a fair and just society." And, if you think lying leaders are equitable then we did well—because lying to Americans regarding economic stability, illegal immigration, terrorism, Iranian nuclear proliferation, and societal moral norms was propagated to further "a fair, just and tolerant society."

Of tolerance, I recall when the government, corporate and even medical institutions began to teach the "doctrine of tolerance" as if it was some "new revelation." And now we are seeing and experiencing the fruit of it, first hand. Sadly, the more men try to follow the "doctrine of tolerance" the more the world races towards an instability that will ultimately bring catastrophic repercussions.

Interestingly, tolerance in the form of patience, forbearance, and charity is part of God's Human Rights laws. In fact, the Lord's motto is, "as much as possible live peaceably with all men."

Furthermore, this whole concept of an Open Society is not original. The idea of one blood, one people who live in harmony and have their being from one God is not new— God, Himself established this foundational concept through Moses who, in turn, conveyed it when he penned the first five books of the Bible. This same ideal is portrayed through Paul in the writing of the New Testament when he addresses philosophers and scholars of religion on Mars Hill in Athens, Greece. He wrote,

> For as I passed by, and beheld your devotions, I found an altar with this inscription, To the Unknown God. . ..Him I declare unto you. God that made the world and all things therein, seeing that he is Lord of heaven and

earth, dwells not in temples made with hands: neither is worshipped with men's hands, as though he needed anything, seeing he gives to all life, breath, and all things: And has made of one blood all nations of men for to dwell on all the face of the earth, and has determined the time before appointed, and the bounds of their habitation: that they should seek the Lord, if haply they might feel after him, and find him, though he be not far from every one of us: For in him we live, and move, and have our being: as certain also of your own poets have said, For we are also his offspring.[127]

Before we move on, I am asking you to go back and re-read what Paul wrote. You may have just skimmed this paragraph; yet, the eternal truths it emphasizes are truly staggering to ponder. Here are a couple of insights to consider:

Firstly, "He has made of one blood all nations" means that, "all men (and women) are made in the image of God," and for that undisputed reason, men (and women) have been given inalienable or God-given rights of which, the right to be respected exists regardless of culture, religion, or social status.

Secondly, in conjunction with inalienable rights, God has appointed the bounds and boundaries of every individual's habitation. In other words, the boundaries of nation states, peoples, cultures, etc. have been set apart by God. And, no matter what those natural national borders are, every individual still lives, moves, and has its being in Him. This means that there should be no boundaries of class, but equal opportunity; no limits on achievement, for all things are possible with God; and, above all, no limits on vision, for God has given to every man a future and a hope called destiny. It is sad when people use their God-given authority to steal this truth from their citizens.

So along with physical national boundaries, God also established boundaries between man and man and between man and God. These limitations should be respected, not removed. As we have seen, teaching tolerance in place of moral character (which Soros defines as "the boundaries of intolerance") has not worked.

Let's look at Soros' explanation of tolerance and intolerance:

Unlimited tolerance must lead to the disappearance of tolerance. If we extend unlimited tolerance even to those who are intolerant, if we are not prepared to defend a tolerant society against the onslaught of the intolerant, then the tolerant will be destroyed, and tolerance with them. In this formulation, I do not imply, for instance, that we should always suppress the utterance of intolerant philosophies; as long as we can counter them by rational argument and keep them in check by public opinion, suppression would certainly be most unwise. But we should claim the *right* to suppress them if necessary even by force; for it may easily turn out that they are not prepared to meet us on the level of rational argument but begin by denouncing all argument; they may forbid their followers to listen to rational argument, because it is deceptive, and teaches them to answer arguments by the use of their fists or pistols. We should, therefore, claim, in the name of tolerance, the right not to tolerate the intolerant. We should claim that any movement preaching intolerance places itself outside the law, and we should consider incitement to intolerance and persecution as criminal, in the same way as we should consider incitement to murder, or to kidnapping, or to the revival of the slave trade, as criminal.[128]

Now, let's sum up what you just read.

Firstly, Soros is not using the word "tolerance" as an adjective—a word or phrase that describes an attribute of a noun—i.e. the man is tolerant. It may look like an adjective, act like one, and smell like one, but it is not one. The word "tolerance" is a noun, meaning that it falls into the category of being a person, place or thing. And that "thing" is an idea. An idea that must accept and include "all philosophy" even if its intent is to subvert an established belief system.

Secondly, if you disagree with that view, you are intolerant. And a society of tolerance has the right to "suppress the intolerant by force" and the "right not to tolerate the intolerant." The intolerant is the worst of deceivers because they may teach their followers to answer with fists or pistols, not a rational argument. Any movement that preaches "intolerance" is outside the law. It is a criminal act that should be punishable in the same manner as murder, kidnapping, or the leader of a slave trade ring.

Soros believes that creating a tolerant society means, compromising conscience by removing all social, personal, moral or ethical convictions. Simply put, removing all personal boundaries. Once accomplished, under what flag of patriotism or identity does one live? And if the nation adopts immigrants or refugees of another religion or political idea that are intolerant to tolerance— i.e. the moral breakdown of society, what does a nation do?

Alan Dershowitz underscores this summation in his observation of how the United Nations International Human Rights Council perpetuates the notion that Israel is an apartheid state (a racially segregated state) while disregarding the real victims of apartheid.

We do have apartheid around the world today. We have it in Saudi Arabia where there is gender apartheid and religious apartheid. We have it in other places and yet, the word is reserved now for Israel which is one of the most diverse and heterogeneous countries not only in the world but the history of the world. You have people of every shade of color, every shade of ethnic background, different kinds of religions living together—often in harmony, in more harmony than in many other countries of the world and yet, the word of apartheid is thrown around. It is such an insult to the victims of apartheid. Mandela and others would be turning over in their graves if he heard the word apartheid used by people like Bishop Tutu and Jimmy Carter who falsely describe Israel today.

He further illustrates the bias of the Human Rights Commission as chaired by those who are the worst human right offenders:

So the great tragedy is that the human rights that were being developed after WWII by people like Delano Roosevelt and others are now being used as a form of discrimination against the nation-state of the Jewish people. . ..We have to fight it at every turn. We can never allow these charges to remain unrebutted. The very people that today are throwing gay people off roofs, who are discriminating against women, discriminating and murdering and raping Christians claiming that they are the standard-bearers of human rights; human rights commission chaired by some of the worst human rights offenders. . ..we must turn that around. . ..I will never stop protesting how the Human Rights agenda is being turned on its head and how it is being used not only to attack a country that has a good human rights record but also to protect countries where mass atrocities are occurring like Syria.

There is no clearer reality than this. Tolerance exercised without a clear sense of right and wrong destroys the human conscience, its judgment, and moral boundaries. The United Nations, in the name of "tolerance" blatantly allows nations who hold the most atrocious human rights records to chair the Human Rights Council.

ॐ

Donald Trump

Many Americans think that Donald Trump is OCD on the issues of borders, national security and the upholding of the America's Declaration and Constitution as our belief system.

Unlike Soros, Trump believes in a patriotic and nationalistic worldview. It is impossible for me to describe America like Soros' as a "closed society." No, instead I must say that America is the real "open society." We do not want to be so tolerant that another religion or ideology can infiltrate and take over our nation! Why? Because we are the only society in the world that attracts the attention of the world's citizens who want to and dream of coming to America.

Donald Trump's worldview is not isolation, of which the media has claimed. But it is one where the truth of boundaries (national and personal), contribute to a just and equitable society. His worldview is non-negotiable when compromise means abandoning the American belief system rooted in the Declaration of Independence and the Constitution of the United States of America! He believes that these are the foundational truths that made America great and will make America Great Again.

Now that we've laid out the developments and sources surrounding the Washington Web, let's look at a few issues vital to America's interests and squirming with vipers. Are you ready? Then make sure you buckle your seat belt!

ഇ

CHAPTER SEVEN

Another Law

"The men that were at peace with thee have deceived thee, and prevailed against thee." Obadiah 1:7

ॐ

I am sure you have heard the term Sharia law in the context of the "war on terrorism," coverage of ISIS, and even from the Oval Office. Under the previous two administrations there was increased support from the White House and staff for the integration of Sharia law within, not only Muslim communities but also the judicial branch of the U.S. government. So, let me ask, what does that mean for you? What is Sharia law and what place should it hold within American society and most of all within the U.S. government?

Truthfully, I could answer all these questions in one paragraph, so we could quickly move onto another issue, stealth jihad. But, that would leave some of you more concerned and confused than educated.

So, let's begin our discussion by talking about what Sharia law is not. It is not a religion or religious law. Many equate the Qur'an and Sharia law to the Torah and Old Testament law. Nothing could be farther from the truth. In fact, they are not even on the same planet in comparatives. But, because of this misperception in the minds of leaders and citizens alike, Sharia law is not only being classified as the religious law of Muslims, but it is being afforded consideration and rights under the First Amendment to the United States Constitution. So, if it is not religious law, what is it?

The term "Sharia" means, "pathway" or simply "path." That means that Sharia law is a set of laws that define "a path." What could that path be? A political path. A socio-economic path. A legal path. A relationship path. A religious path. A jihad path. Or simply—A path. Some may say it's a true path, a right path, the only path. Others will say it's a false path, a destructive path, the wrong path. But for most, they just see it as a "foreign, religious path."

The body of Sharia law originates from several documents including the Qur'an, which Muslims believe is the "uncreated" word of Allah as dictated to the prophet Mohammed; the hadiths which are the sayings of Mohammed; and agreed upon interpretations by Islamic scholars.[129]

According to *The foundations of Islamic Studies* by Dr.Abu Ameenah Bilal Philips, Module 2 Tafseer, the Qur'an is:

> The words of God, revealed in Arabic, in a rhythmical form, to the prophet. Its recitation is used in forms of worship. . ..The hadiths are the words of God according to the words of Mohammed in Arabic. They are not used in worship but can give details on proper worship.[130]

Now all that sounds harmless, doesn't it? I agree. So, let's dig a little further.

Hear what the Center of Security Policy writes in its mini course on Sharia law:

> Sharia is a totalitarian ideology that controls all aspects of life. All are forced to submit to Islamic law as defined by theologians. Sharia institutionalizes discrimination against women, deprives people of freedom of expression and association, criminalizes sexual freedom, and incites hatred and violence against people of certain social groups. As manifested in countries officially ruled by Islamic law, Sharia condones or commands abhorrent behavior, including underage and forced marriage, "honor killing" (usually of women and girls) to preserve family "honor," female genital mutilation, polygamy and domestic abuse, and even marital rape.

As someone who has studied and written about Islamic law and jihad, I can tell you that what you just read is only the tip of the iceberg when it comes to the depth in which Sharia law encroaches upon, controls, and violates human rights laws. And within Sharia law there is a "no tolerance" edict for democratic law and the United States Constitution. Why?

As we have discussed already in chapters four and five, the United States Constitution is the bridge between the Declaration of Independence and the covenant George Washington made with God over the founding of America. So, unlike Europe where Sharia law conflicts with democracy and Human Rights; in the United States the struggle between Sharia and the Constitution is over whose God is the true God and whose laws are more righteous. This is serious stuff folks. Every, and I mean every, liberty afforded by God under the protection of the Constitution is being challenged—and I bet many Americans are not aware of this, you think?

There is a concept in Islam called "jahiliyyah." Jahiliyyah means "ignorance of God's divine guidance in the earth." This term is intimately connected to the propagation of Sharia law. Unlike the gospel which is "good news" and redemptive in nature, Islamists believe that the whole world is in a state of "jahiliyyah" (ignorance and unbelief toward God) and therefore, it is the responsibility of Islamists to bring the world out of the state of "ignorance."[131] This is accomplished through jihad and the imputing of Sharia law upon all aspects of life.[132]

ဆ

The Constitution's Archenemy

Serious questions are being raised about the compatibility of Sharia law and the Constitution of the United States of America. And they should be. One of the most significant differences between Sharia law and the Constitution are the three "freedoms" afforded by the First Amendment: Freedom of religion, freedom of speech, and freedom of dissent. All three of these freedoms are forbidden, subservient, and/or a violation worthy of death, under Sharia law.

On religion Sharia law states:

"Those who reject Islam must be killed. If they turn back (from Islam), take hold of them and kill them wherever you find them." Qur'an 4:89; "Whoever changed his [Islamic] religion, then kill him" Sahih al-Bukhari, 9:84:57. Sharia law enforces dhimmi status (second-class citizen, apartheid-type laws) on non-Muslims, prohibiting them from observing their religious practices publicly, building or repairing churches, raising their voices during prayer or ringing church bells; if dhimmi laws are violated in the Sharia State, penalties are those used for prisoners of war:

death, slavery, release or ransom. (o9.14, o11.0-o11.11, Umdat al-Salik).[133]

The Second Amendment of the Constitution grants the Right to Bear Arms. If Sharia law were to usurp Constitutional law or have its way in America, all non-Muslims would be forbidden to possess firearms. This leads one to consider the roots behind a lot of the opposition to gun control.

The Fifth, Sixth and Seventh Amendments deal with the right of due process and a fair trial. Under Sharia law, there is no justice or due process of law. Just witnesses and testimonies. Take for example, the Hadith Sahih al-Bukhari which states that Mohammed said, "No Muslim should be killed for killing a Kafir (infidel)." Also, non-Muslims are prohibited from testifying against Muslims and a woman's testimony is equal to half of a man's. So much for equity or equality.

The Eighth Amendment of the Constitution states that the government cannot inflict "cruel or unusual punishment." This is not the case under Sharia law. Sharia supports punishments that are barbaric: "Cut off the hands of thieves, whether they are male or female, as punishment for what they have done—a deterrent from Allah." Qur'an 5:38; A raped woman is punished: "The woman and the man guilty of adultery or fornication—flog each of them with a hundred stripes" (Sura 24:2).

Lastly, the Fourteenth Amendment calls for the right to equal protection and due process. Under Sharia law all non-Muslims are dhimmis. Under dhimmi law, existing today in modern Sharia states, Jews, Christians, and other non-Muslims are not equal to Muslims before the law. Under Sharia law, women, girls, apostates, homosexuals and "blasphemers" are all denied equality.

Now, let's sum up Sharia law: anti-American, anti-constitutional, anti-democratic, and anti-human rights. So, is there anything good about it? Yes, as a matter of fact, there is.

Recently, in speaking with a friend who worked as a diplomat for the United Nations, I learned that the representatives that fight the hardest for morality within International law were the Muslims. My friend noted that the lack of values within the United Nations was self-evident in the decisions and heinous acts of control and negotiated policy. "There is no moral consideration to the agenda or policy" and "it's the Muslims that stand their moral grounds."

With that said, what Sharia law is doing for the Western world is causing it to rethink its nihilistic illusions—that a democracy can exist without God and that human rights can be regulated without moral values. It underscores and highlights how far America has strayed from God; the Constitution, and its moral foundation; which without, a righteous nation cannot survive. Need we be reminded that God said, "all the nations that forget (reject) God shall be turned into Hell."[134] And if America is not on the edge of hell right now, I don't know where it is. The good news is that we are just on the edge—there is still time for an about face!

Now, let's turn our attention on how Sharia law is infiltrating into the fabric of America. Ready?

ഇ

ObamaCare: Sharia's Door

Throughout the eight years of the Obama administration, the supremacy of the U.S. Constitution was at the forefront of debate in almost every federal undertaking of change beginning with the institution of ObamaCare (ACA—Affordable Care Act)—an organism upholding the right of all citizens to have affordable health care. A fundamental human right.

As a health care bill, very few argued that it was not needful nor an aid in meeting a basic human right, the right to life. But what else was in the bill we didn't know. As Nancy Pelosi so eloquently said, "We are going to have to pass the bill to find out what is in it."[135] The statement was laughable then, but in retrospect, no one is laughing now. What started out as "meeting the needs of a basic human right" is now categorized as an overreach of the federal government of historic proportions.[136]

The health care bill not only questions individual and employer mandates, but also the legitimate use of American taxes and the expansion of Medicaid. Due to the size of the bill alone—initially 1,990[137] pages and now hovering around 20,000[138] pages, few have read it in its entirety. And those who have read the document found gross abuses of constitutional rights and tax allocations.[139][140][141]

Regarding the ACA tax code amendment surrounding individual mandate and the expansion of Medicaid, a federal lawsuit *"National Federation of Independent Business v. Sebelius"*[142] was filed against the federal government in 2010. Twenty-six states filed the lawsuit along with Mary Brown, Kaj Ahlburg, and the National Federation of Independent Business.[143]

The Supreme Court ruled to uphold the tax amendment and Medicaid expansion, as stated in the ACA, in a 5-4 decision. The dissenting Justices Scalia, Kennedy, Thomas, and Alito argued that "The individual mandate represented an unprecedented abuse of federal power, for the federal government never before used the Commerce Clause to compel entry into Commerce." And the individual mandate was not a legitimate exercise of the power to tax because the statute described the fine as a "penalty" rather than a tax. They concluded that the Affordable Care Act should be overturned in its entirety, as it could not function as intended without the individual mandate.[144]

Another challenge to ObamaCare reflected on the overreaching arm of the federal government into the religious and faith-based communities. The overreach is highlighted in the case, *Burwell vs. Hobby Lobby* who was granted a writ of certiorari in November of 2013. At the core of the issue, was the defining of 'mandatory contraception' to be included in the health care packages offered to employees of such institutions as, non-for-profit organizations or for-profit faith-based businesses. Hobby Lobby saw this clause as moral infringement, not because of "contraception" per se, as birth control pills and other devices used to prevent pregnancy are within the scope of acceptable health insurance coverage. The conflict of conscience arose over the definition of "contraception" that included immediate and later term abortion pills and aids. In the eyes of Hobby Lobby, as well as many other religious institutions and faith-based companies, this inclusion directly defied both moral conscience and moral law, "Thou shall not murder." It also broke the First Amendment and the Religious Freedom Restoration Act (RFRA) enacted in 1993. The RFRA stated that the federal government, "shall not substantially burden a person's exercise of religion even if the burden results from a rule of general applicability."[145]

The Supreme Court voted in favor of Hobby Lobby and all associated cases making it not mandatory to adhere to this clause as a faith-based business.

In her dissent, Justice Ruth Bader Ginsburg argued precedent from the case *Employment Division, Department of Human Resources of Oregon vs. Smith.* The Court upheld that "there is no violation of the freedom of religion when an infringement on that right is merely an incidental consequence of an otherwise valid statute."

The law firm that represented Hobby Lobby, the Becket Fund for Religious Liberty, has a docket of cases due to government overreach on sensitive issues such as contraception, and same-sex marriage: "We find there has been an aggressive push from the government to become the sole arbiter of morality, which is not good for our country," said executive director Kristina Arriaga. "Regrettably, religious liberty work has augmented exponentially."[146]

Following the Hobby Lobby case, there was a wave of fear that emerged in chat rooms and social media over the possibility that "the court's ruling on the Hobby Lobby case" could indeed serve as a stepping stone for Sharia law.

Here is one response posted on the Liberal forum:

Based upon the ruling of current Supreme Court case, religious rights and government regulations shall be clearly identified as it relates to the commerce clause or federal authority. So, should the pro-life and anti-birth control lobby get "their way" on ObamaCare?

Given our Constitution, what is to say a Muslim business owner could use religion to require that all female employees wear burkas or face coverings?[147]

George Takai, a gay rights activist and actor best known for his role as Hikaru Sulu, in the television series Star Trek, was interviewed by *Froward Progressives.* During his interview, he also asked the question, "What if Muslims owned Hobby Lobby and tried imposing Sharia law on employees?"[148]

ℰℐ

The Growing Sharia Narrative

Around the same time of the filing of the *Burwell vs. Hobby Lobby* case (2013), there was heightened awareness and growing concern throughout American society about the encroachment of Sharia law in government; and more specifically about the Patient Protection Affordable Care Act (PPACA). One of the reasons for such was the wording around the religious clauses found within the healthcare bill.

Since 2010, there had been rumors that the word "dhimmitude" was on page 107 of H.R. 3590 of the PPACA. This was held to be true in the original document, but due to outrage from the faith-based communities, the word "dhimmitude" was said to be subsequently removed. Whether this rumor was true (it does appear that Snopes fact checker originally stated that the word was in the document in 2010 and then changed its position statement in 2013) or not, the damage was done. Following this claim, the word "dhimmitude" became a hot metadata keyword filling emails, websites, and commentaries. Below is one example of an email paragraph that was circulated about the insertion of "dhimmitude."

> ObamaCare allows the establishment of dhimmitude and Sharia Muslim diktat in the United States. Muslims are specifically exempted from the government mandate to purchase insurance, and also from the penalty tax for being uninsured. Islam considers insurance to be 'gambling,' 'risk-taking,' and 'usury' and is thus banned. Muslims are specifically granted an exemption based on this.[149]

> How convenient. So, I, as a Christian will have crippling IRS liens placed against all of my assets, including real estate, cattle, and even accounts receivable, and will face hard prison time because I refuse to buy insurance or pay the penalty tax. Meanwhile, Louis Farrakhan will have no such penalty and will have 100% of his health insurance paid for by the de facto government insurance. Non-Muslims will be paying a tax to subsidize Muslims. This is dhimmitude.

Alas this is just one of many email chains that circulated throughout the country between 2010 and 2013.

Although numerous political fact checking sites have debunked the claim that the word dhimmitude is in ObamaCare, there is substantial evidence that the "concern" of Sharia laws growing influence within American Society are founded.

In 2011, Erica Burns wrote a stellar article entitled, *"Muslim Exempt from ObamaCare?"*[150] In the article, he clarifies the rumors circulating over the word "dhimmitude" and shares his assessment that, Muslim exception from paying for Healthcare "won't play out." He cites the reasons for this under the Individual mandate.

> Under Subtitle F, Part I, Section 1501—the individual responsibility requirement to maintain minimum essential coverage—individuals must be "a member of a recognized religious sect" that doesn't participate in Social Security. . ..The religious exemption applies to any person who is a member of a "recognized religious sect or division" with "established tenets or teachings" that would forbid that person from accepting public or private insurance.

He continues his analysis by noting that at first glance, it appears that Muslims would be able to take advantage of the religious exemption clause because most American Muslims affiliate with a "recognized religious sect" and the strict interpretation of the Qur'an "forbids the acceptance of public or private insurance." However, if you pay Social Security taxes or receive Social Security benefits, you are disqualified from the exemption. But, if the community sets up what is called a "health care sharing ministry" for its members, they would be eligible.[151]

ℰↃ

Takaful – What?

A "Health Care Sharing Ministry" what exactly is that? Simply put, it is a non-profit religious organization in which members contribute money to cover the medical expenses of those in need. And once established, those who contribute to the organization become exempt from the requirement to purchase health insurance.[152]

Since ObamaCare, hundreds of health sharing ministries have popped up throughout Christian communities, but among Muslim communities, something else emerged.

Health Care Sharing Ministries, which have existed for more than twenty years in America, "exemplify the Muslim principle of *Takaful*—individuals cooperating and protecting one another against loss or damage."[153] And, even though Health Care Sharing Ministries do not appear to be the chosen path of Takaful for healthcare in America, Takaful is being realized through another venue, Sharia-compliant insurance products.

Since December 1, 2008, AIG Commercial Insurance started offering insurance "compliant with key Islamic finance tenets and based on the concept of mutual insurance." [154] Interestingly, the insurance(s) is underwritten by a subsidiary of AIG, Risk Specialists Insurance, Inc., in conjunction with Lexington Insurance Co. and AIG Takaful Enaya—headquartered in Bahrain. According to the Insurance Journal, "AIG Takaful Enaya is licensed by the Central Bank of Bahrain and its Sharia Supervisory Board is composed of Sharia scholars Sheikh Nizam Yaquby, Dr. Mohammed Ali Elgari and Dr. Muhammad Imran Usmani." At the time of this writing, the AIG website for Bahrain and Bahrain Takaful was not available; although, all its other global websites were operational. And if you google AIG, there are no results for Bahrain or AIG Takaful Enaya.

Takaful extends far beyond its primary definition "individuals cooperating and protecting one another against loss or damage." It is an arm of Sharia compliance that has grave implications within Western Society— although not apparent on the surface.

The Islamic Finance News cites the following:

In 1974, the National Religious Council issued a legal opinion that conventional life insurance is not permissible because it contains elements of (1) risk and uncertainty; (2) gambling; and (3) interest. Hence, in 1985, the Grand Council of Islamic Scholars in Saudi Arabia (the Majma al-Fiqh) approved the Takaful system as the alternative form of insurance written in compliance with Islamic Sharia.[155] The Grand Council approved Takaful as a system of co-operation and mutual help for the good of society by the Grand Council.

Insurance, as a concept, is just developing within Muslim communities worldwide. Before Takaful insurance, it was perceived that Sharia law prohibited the use of insurance because such products employed interest and risk forbidden by Sharia law. The institution of insurance within Muslim society has been a slow process, one that began in the 1970s.

Today, Takaful insurance companies see their Takaful products and services as ethically based and therefore believe that they will also appeal to non-Muslims.[156][157]

സ

Takaful Expanded

Another area that falls under Takaful and is in direct opposition to the American lending practices is Sharia compliant mortgage loans.

Sharia law forbids Muslims to pay interest on loans. Therefore, non-interest-bearing loans must be part of the package.[158]

Of Sharia compliant mortgage loans and increased compliance to Sharia law within Western Society, Dr.

Andre Bostom says, "Such dangerously misguided efforts kowtow to, and abet, Islamic supremacism."[159]

Bostom looks to Sayyid Maududi, a 20th-century Islamic thinker, to validate his statement. In his book *"The Economic Problem of Man and its Islamic Solution,"* Maududi outlines the economic ills of the world and how neither communism or fascism, nor national-socialism can solve them. He states that only through Islam are all financial burdens lightened and economic evils resolved. He emphasizes how that, in every sphere of global commerce involving trade and, in every social sphere that extends to civil services, army, and judicial proceedings, Islam has "lightened a very great economic burden from society."[160]

Maududi underscores his summary with this statement, "This economic system has a 'deep relationship' with the political, judicial, legal, cultural and social system of Islam."[161] All of which are "fundamentally based on the moral system of Islam." Maududi is also very quick to tie the moral system held within each of these societal underpinnings to its dependency on one's belief in an all-powerful and all-knowing God and one's sense of responsibility to Him."[162]

Maududi concludes with an admonition that demanded not only Muslim acceptance, but also that of the whole world, "If you do not accept this creed, this moral system and the whole of this code of life (i.e. Sharia law), completely as it is, the economic system of Islam, divorced from its source (God), cannot be maintained or administered in its purity for even a single day, nor will any appreciable advantage accrue from it if you take it out of its wider context and then seek to apply [it] to your life."[163]

From the statements of Maududi, we see that Bostom's perspective accurately asserts that the advancement of financial tools within Western society is a grave cause of concern.

Of Sharia-compliant mortgages, Bostom concludes, "Sharia-compliant mortgages, and all aspects of so-called Sharia-compliant finance, should be rejected because they are vehicles for the promulgation of Islamic law, an integrated religious-political system antithetical to our most fundamental Western freedoms."[164]

Thus far, we have discussed how the institution of the Patient Protection Affordable Care Act opened doors for the awareness of Sharia law and for Muslims to seek alternative measures to meet their healthcare and overall insurance needs within the confines of Sharia law—adhering to Takaful.

ℬ

Radical Departure

Along with the societal changes that accompanied the Affordable Care Act, was a radical departure from the government narrative that connected Islam with terrorism.

This departure was also seen in the semantic differences between Sharia law and the Constitution. At this point, it must be noted that when President Obama took office there already was a growing pro-Muslim narrative being cultivated within the Bush administration.

President George Bush, following September 11th, adopted not only the 'war on terror' narrative but, also, a policy of appeasement toward Muslim communities within America. It was his intent to thwart any racial backlash following the terrorist attack by Islamists on American soil. To accomplish such, the President took a very pro-American Muslim position following the 9-11 attack which included putting the leaders of Muslim organizations into the limelight. Additionally, the Muslim communities and agencies themselves became pro-active through giving blood and attending national memorials and Christian events to show their support.

On September 14, 2001, three days after the attacks, a National Day of Prayer and Remembrance ceremony was held at the National Cathedral in Washington, D.C. This memorial service, attended by the President, emphasized healing and unity. It was televised and hosted numerous Washington diplomats including members of Congress. An opening prayer was given by Dr. Muzammil H. Siddiqi, president of the Indiana-based Islamic Society of North America (ISNA). He was the first to read the Qur'an in a National Day of Prayer service. Other leaders representing Islamic institutions such as Leaders of the

American Muslim Political Coordination Council (AMPCC), Council on American-Islamic Relations (CAIR) and the Muslim Brotherhood (MB) were present to give condolences. In fact, the very afternoon of 9-11, the President had scheduled a meeting with the AMPCC and a coalition of American-Muslim leaders to discuss a new Middle East Peace initiative.

American backlash was immediate and severe. There were attacks on Muslims and Islamic institutions throughout the country. To counteract further American hostility, President Bush publicly heightened his support for the Muslim community. On September 17, he visited a Mosque and held an hour-long meeting at Washington D.C.'s Islamic Center. The meeting surveyed a lot of topics of which one was, "the need for American Muslim input on government policy."[165]

Subsequently, the President gave a press conference where he was given a "copy of the Qur'an and Paul Findley's book, *Silent No More: Confronting America's False Images of Islam*." Notably, Paul Findley was a Republican with a strong propensity towards the Palestinian plight, and for forging communications with the Palestine Liberation Organization.[166]

On September 20th, President Bush addressed a joint session of Congress. In his speeches, he condemned the violence against Muslims as un-American and shameful. He also reframed the Islamic narrative: "Osama Bin

Laden and his cohorts had "hijacked" Islam itself"—the otherwise peaceful religion. The effect was immediate. Violence and hate crimes dropped 95% that same day.

On September 26th, President Bush held another meeting with Muslim leaders, inviting those who had been stranded overseas due to the attacks. In this session, he etched in stone the new narrative the White House was going to adopt toward Islam: "Islam and their religion stand for 'goodness and peace.'" Unfortunately, the President's position was doing irrevocable damage to the American Muslims—by not making a distinction between moderate Muslims and Islamists, President Bush was encouraging, even facilitating, stealth jihad (discussed in chapter eight).

The distinction between American Muslims and Islamists is stark. American Muslims are, at most, traditional in their religious practice, American in their political aspirations, and secular in their daily lifestyles; while practicing Islamists are Muslims that adhere to Sharia law in their personal and community lives. They believe that Sharia law should be the ultimate Law of the land. They also support Islamic charities, education and foreign entities affiliated to terrorist organizations.

With this narrative in place, President Obama was positioned to begin redefining America's domestic and worldview towards Islam, thus opening the door for Sharia law to rapidly infiltrate into the fabric of American society. Let's move on to see exactly how President

Obama and Islam continued undermining America—through Stealth Jihad.

៩០

*"The Constitution is the guide which
I never will abandon."*

George Washington

೮౨

CHAPTER EIGHT

Stealth Jihad

"Do you know Abner the son of Ner, that he came to deceive you, and to know your going out and your coming in, and to know all that you do." 2 Samuel 3:25

&

Now that we have looked at Sharia law and the emergence of *Takaful* since Obamacare, let's turn our attention to the method Islamists are using to gain dominance in America through Sharia law: stealth jihad.

"Stealth what?" you might ask. Stealth is a word more familiar to you than you think. It's such a cool way of saying, "secret" or "hidden." It's like the word Trojan. You say Trojan and anyone who knows Greek history thinks of the Trojan horse built as a gift for a king; and when the horse was delivered to the city gates of the King—surprise! An army jumped out and overtook the city. That is some serious betrayal and deception going on—a gift in the one hand and the sword in the other.

Stealth jihad is the same concept. It is an infiltration or takeover of a nation through hidden, secret and subversive agendas. "Stealth" is defined as "secret, hidden," while "jihad," in its most basic sense, means "struggle." In Islamic law, jihad is "the struggle against the infidels (the unbelievers) and the struggle to rule the world through the institution of Islamic law."[167] And, that struggle can take on covert and overt manifestations.

Overt expressions are what we see and read about in the daily news: terrorism and incitement against a nation such as Israel—as seen in the BDS Movement (Boycott, Divestment, and Sanctions).

Covert manifestations, on the other hand, are not readily detectable. However, they do surface in various ways; first and foremost, in money trails. They also show up in lawsuits, judicial compromise, the appearance of Mosques as well as cluster Islamic communities as and NGO organizations that fund anti-Israel agendas and terrorism. Most importantly, there is the infiltration of Islamic centered individuals and organizations into key political positions.

And, no matter how American a Muslim is, if he adheres strictly to Islamic law he cannot remain neutral about democracy and the United States Constitution, as they are an affront to Islam. Therefore, he or she will directly or indirectly aid in its overthrow. Time is not of the essence, only the goal. And the goal for every devout Islamist is to strategically move the chess board pieces until they put the American government in checkmate.

ℰꝋ

A New Narrative

Language does matter when drawing clear lines between good and evil, i.e. terrorism. With that said, the Obama administration not only continued the Bush narrative of Muslim good will, but they took it one step further by removing language that may be offensive to Muslims and dropping Bush's 'war on terror' along with any and all narratives that associated Muslims with terrorism.

In 2011, Deputy Attorney General James Cole confirmed that the Obama administration was "pulling back all training materials used for law enforcement and national security communities, in order to eliminate all references to Islam."[168] This decision came after a 2009 indictment of 5 Muslim's in the *Holy Land Foundation* terrorist finance trial. The trial did more than disclose the funneling of $12 million to Hamas; it also revealed the government's diverse views of Islam, terrorism, and Muslims. Upon hearing the Muslim references in the training manuals, there was an outcry from CAIR and other Muslim Brotherhood front groups, even though all these groups identified as having connections to Hamas in the trial.

This marked yet another phase of escalating Muslim advocacy over the Islamic narrative. Salam al-Marayati, President of Muslim Public Affairs Council (MPAC), threatened the FBI, in a Los Angeles Times op-ed. He demanded that all "bigoted and inflammatory views" on Muslims be removed from all law enforcement training manuals. His Op-Ed cites a few examples such as, "'devout' Muslims are more prone toward violence, Islam 'aims to transform a country's culture into 7th-century Arabian ways', the Islamic charitable giving is a 'funding mechanism of combat,' and Mohammed was a "violent cult leader."[169] It also called for the Justice Department and the FBI to apologize and establish an 'interagency task force' to review training material and select trainers.

Furthermore, in his Op-Ed, Marayati cited a 2010 presentation by an analyst working for a U.S. attorney's office in Pennsylvania:

'Civilization Jihad' stretching back from the dawn of Islam and waged today in the U.S. by 'civilians, juries, lawyers, media, academia, and charities who threaten 'our values.' The goal of that war: 'Replacement of American Judeo-Christian and Western liberal social, political, and religious foundations of Islam.[170]

This baseless statement, per Marayati, is at the heart of the goal of Islamic law, according to Maududi. What and who Marayati cites is of critical importance in understanding the depth of what he is attacking. It was far more than training material or inflammatory words. It was American values and ideology.

Salam Marayati was not without warrant in his Op-Ed, as he also attributes the Muslim community and its cooperation with law enforcement to the thwarting of at least 40% of terrorist attacks in America. On the other hand, the tone, threats and calculated inclusions of the Op-Ed earmarked a more serious development—intimidation works within the White House.

The Obama administration's response to Marayati and other Muslim advocacy groups demands was irrational—a sign of government capitulation. It can be summed up with the statement of Dwight Holton, the U.S. Attorney in Oregon:

> I want to be perfectly clear about this: training materials that portray Islam as a religion of violence or with a tendency towards violence are wrong, they are offensive, and they are contrary to everything that this President, this Attorney General and the Department of Justice stand for and they will not be tolerated. The training materials pose a significant threat to National Security because they play into a false narrative propagated by terrorists that the United States is at war with Islam.[171]

This political move to change the training manuals was the beginning of the end of America's fight against Islam. It escalated the anti-Islam terrorist narrative and even led to a purge of Pentagon documents that mentioned Islam. Furthermore, terrorism on American soil was reduced to hate crimes.

ଞ

Hate Crimes or Terrorism?

One of the most noticeable outcomes of the Obama administration's push to remove the term "Islam" from its association to terrorism or anti-American policy, is the government's response to terrorist attacks on American soil. Between 2008 and 2016, there was a minimum of fourteen known terrorist attacks in America resulting in 94 deaths and 368 wounded. In addition to terrorist attacks, seven recorded Sharia law honor killings resulting in 13 deaths.[172] In every instance, the appropriate narrative for a terrorist attack or honor killing was reduced to that of an individual psychopath and hate crime.

According to the Hate Crime Data Collection Guidelines, a Hate Crime is defined as, "A criminal offense committed against a person or property which is motivated, in whole or in part, by the offender's bias against a race, religion, disability, sexual orientation, or ethnicity, national origin; also known as a Hate Crime."[173]

Terrorism, on the other hand, is defined by the FBI as "a federal crime of terrorism; an offense that is calculated to influence or affect the conduct of government by intimidation or coercion." It also means to "retaliate against government conduct; and is a violation of one of the several listed statutes, including § 930(c) (relating to killing or attempted killing during an attack on a federal facility with a dangerous weapon); and § 1114 (relating to killing or attempted killing of officers and employees of the U.S.)."[174]

In addition to this broad definition of terrorism, the FBI attributed three characteristics to "domestic terrorism:"

- Acts dangerous to human life that violates federal or state law;

- Acts intended (i) to intimidate or coerce a civilian population; (ii) to influence the policy of a government by intimidation or coercion; or (iii) to affect the conduct of a government by mass destruction, assassination. or kidnapping; and,

- Acts that occur primarily within the territorial jurisdiction of the United States.

This aversion to tell the truth and mislead the American people did not gone unnoticed. Responsively, former U.S. Representative Michelle Bachman remarked, "The Obama administration and its surrogates constantly act as the chief defenders of Islam, falling all over themselves to protect it from criticism after each new jihadist attack on America and Europe."

Her comment came after an outrage from a community in Idaho where a 5-year-old special needs girl was allegedly covered in urine, raped, and made to drink urine. The perpetrators were teenage and younger refugees from Sudan and Iraq. The government initially tried to cover up this incident. Subsequently, following its leak, the Idaho General Attorney Wendy Olson gave a statement that set off a legal uproar over the First Amendment:

> "The spread of false information or inflammatory or threatening statements about the perpetrators or the crime itself reduces public safety and may violate federal law."[175]

In response to Olson's statement, First Amendment attorney, David Yerushalmi said,

> "Ms. Olson's not-so-veiled threat is closer to illegal speech by a government official than the speech she threatens, but this abuse of government power is no surprise coming from the political hacks this president has appointed in the U.S. attorneys' office."

Irony has its place in every facet of life. And the Obama administration was full of it. It's ironic how the more it preached that Islam is a peaceful, just, and compassionate religion the more angry, unjust and non-compassionate the Obama administration became toward its American citizens.

In 2010, there was a compelling case that sparked debate regarding Sharia law. Judge Joseph Charles, a New Jersey family court judge, refused to grant a restraining order to a woman who was being sexually abused by her Muslim Moroccan husband. The judge ruled that the man was behaving according to his Muslim beliefs. And, in the Islamic religion, a woman should submit completely to her husband's will—which includes abusive sexual relations. This decision was overruled by the Appellate Court of New Jersey which held that religious beliefs of the husband were irrelevant to the case and that assault was illegal.[176]

In Oklahoma, the citizens introduced an amendment to the Constitution of Oklahoma, State Question 755, that stated, "The courts shall not look to the legal precepts of other nations or cultures. Specifically, the courts shall not consider international law or Sharia law." [177] This amendment, which was passed with a 70% approval by the electorate in November 2010, was blocked by U.S. District Judge Vicki Miles-LaGrange. Her ruling was subsequently upheld by the Federal 10th Circuit Court of Appeals in Denver on January 10, 2012.

What makes this case so interesting is that the Federal Court blocked it specifically for the use of the words, "Sharia law," twice. Judge LaGrange argued that "singling out Sharia law conveys a message of disapproval of the Muslim faith, and has the effect of inhibiting the Muslim religion."[178]

This attempt to block an overwhelmingly approved Amendment because of its insertion of Sharia law two times is indicative of the influence Muslim organizations had not only within the Obama administration, but also within the Judicial branch. The Constitution does not give the Judiciary branch of government the right to block or veto an amendment made by the people. Silencing the voice of Americans and their guaranteed rights of the First Amendment is being called into question at the highest Judicial level in American courts.

Michael Curtis further elaborates on the liberties of different religions and cultures within the United States. Rabbinical courts can function within Jewish communities and America Indian tribal courts are fully functional. The difference is that these tribunals have not "intruded into the general legal system."[179] But, as noted in the abuse case tried by Judge Charles in New Jersey, Sharia law is attempting to intrude into the American judicial system.

Undoubtedly, Sharia law is not compatible with Constitutional law. And, under the Obama administration, the U.S. government's protection of Sharia and its political correctness over its connection to Islam brought into question the long-standing role of America as a leader in democratic freedoms and its Constitution as the Supreme Law of the land.

Near the end of Obama's presidency, he nominated the first Sharia compliant, Muslim federal judge, Abid Qureshi. He is a Pakistani immigrant who had practiced law in the United States for ten years and was educated at American universities. He has no judicial experience, but he did have "ties to Islamists, which included the Saudi Arabian government."

About Qureshi editor Leo Hohmann writes,[180] "Most troubling for those concerned that Qureshi's allegiance to Islamic law may influence his view of the U.S. Constitution in his work representing a private school with ties to the hardline Saudi Arabian government in a case before the National Labor Relations Board."

Daniel Akbar, a former Sharia lawyer and Islamic expert for the Supreme Court of Iran also weighed in on Obama's nomination of Abid Qureshi:

> An Islamist is one that has an orthodox understanding of Islam. CAIR, ISNA, all have an orthodox understanding of the authoritative Islamic sources. If you have that, then you believe orthodox rules must rule a person's life. . ..If you are pro-even one law of Sharia, you are an Islamist. If you are someone coming from the Middle East and say, 'I don't give a damn about Muhammad and about Islam, but I'm a Muslim,' then you are not a problem. But if you are talking about someone with an orthodox understanding of Islam, then we should have a problem with you being a judge. So, we don't know if Mr. Qureshi is an Islamist or just a Muslim. But since I'm seeing on Twitter that

CAIR and ISNA and all those activists for Sharia are supporting him, I'm suspicious he is an Islamist.[181]

The nomination of Qureshi expired on January 3, 2017 with the 114th Congress. Although he did not replace the seat vacated by Judge Rosemary M. Collyer his nomination set a precedence for future nominations.

Such precedence mandates answers to underlying questions such as: Is the candidate a Muslim or an Islamist? Can he or she objectively interpret the U.S. Constitution? If the White House frowns upon anti-Muslim rhetoric or if the word Islamist cannot to be used or recorded, how would a candidate like Mr. Abid Qureshi be questioned by the U.S. Senate? Would the Senate be able to inquire of the candidate's connections to Islamist organizations? And could they extrapolate vital information regarding the candidate's views on Sharia law without pushback from Muslim groups?

Because Mr. Qureshi was not interviewed by the Senate, these questions still need to be asked and answered by future Muslim judicial candidates. How they play out remains to be seen.

ॐ

Stealth Jihad

The escalating government threats surrounding anti-Muslim rhetoric are a direct infringement upon the First Amendment of the Constitution, "Congress shall not abridge 'the freedom of speech.'" Unfortunately, Congress did not have the opportunity to weigh in on the Islamic-Muslim conundrum. During his tenure, President Obama bypassed the legislative branch and dictated to the Judicial, Military and National Security arms of government rhetoric, norms and laws surrounding Islamic terrorism, Muslim immigration, Muslim refugees, anti-Muslim rhetoric and Sharia law.

Now. let's turn our attention to closing observations on how American democracy is perceived by Islam and subverted through stealth jihad. Such an overview enumerates how and why the Obama administration failed to create a narrative that accurately reflected Islamic Sharia law: a very present threat to the future of Democracy and the Constitution's supremacy within the United States of America.

Sadly, throughout the Obama presidency the demands and threats of the Muslim lobby influenced an intentional narrative from the White House to create an illusion of peace surrounding Islam as a religion. From the onset, Obama placed members of the Muslim Brotherhood into key staff positions. These staff members played a significant role in fashioning Obama's Islamic worldview as well as the legal framework used to persuade Justices to block or violate American Constitutional freedoms, such as presented in the Oklahoma amendment case.

Such actions on behalf of the former President can be understood as contributing to the erosion of Constitutional authority. There were also numerous other lobby capitulations and legal actions under the guise of "human rights" that one can point to, such as the legalization of same-sex marriage, but they are not within the scope of this chapter.

The objective of the Obama presidency and his administration was to ensure the protection of the American Muslim community and reshape the Islamic Muslim image from that of terrorist to one of peace and compatibility. It also intended to disenfranchise terrorism from its Islamic roots and Sharia law. This not only projected a false narrative regarding Islam, but it also failed to address the actual threat that America faces: an ideological threat crouched in stealth Jihad—an internal Jihad working to overthrow the Constitution of the United States of America as the supreme law of the land.

One of the most erroneous claims of Islam is that Sharia law is a religious law and, therefore, it is protected by the First Amendments of the Constitution. However, Sharia law is does not fall under the category of religious law. On the contrary, it is a "totalitarian socio-political doctrine" which places it outside the First Amendment. Sharia means, "the path" and though it has a spiritual component such as prayer five times a day, it possesses a "comprehensive legal and political framework."[182] Patrick Poole, military and law enforcement consultant on antiterrorism issues, and Joseph Schmitz, former Inspector General, Department of Defense remarked, "it would be a mistake to think of Sharia as a "religious" code in the Western sense because it seeks to regulate all manner of behavior in the secular sphere—economic, social, military, legal and political."[183] As evidenced throughout portions of this book, Sharia law is making inroads into each of these channels of civilian life.

The divide and debate within Islam, and among Muslims who hold to tenets of Sharia, appear to be among moderate Muslims who hold Sharia as a code of personal conduct and Muslims who see Sharia as supreme law. Those who see Sharia as supreme law are known as Muslim supremacists or Islamists. It is the latter category that the Obama presidency failed to clearly identify, isolate, and abrogate from the democratic government of the United States.

Islamists, purport a global totalitarian concept of conquest known as a caliphate and Sharia law is their religious-social-political system—a system all Muslims are mandated to uphold, and all Westerners must submit. The method for bringing about their objectives throughout the West is "stealth jihad." For Islamists, "stealth jihad" is a "civil, internal jihad often called 'dawa'—a call to Islam." It characteristically is marked by a non-violent means to infiltrate into government and society.

Tactics utilized to employ "stealth Jihad" are found in the Qur'an under the guise of lying and deceit. Did you know that the Qur'an permits lying and the use of deceit to overthrow an enemy, i.e. America and American democracy? This tactic is known as Taqiyya. In addition, Islamists use other forms of deceit such as Kitman: Lying by omission, Tawriya: Intentionally creating a false impression, and Muruna: 'Blending in' by setting aside some practices of Islam or Sharia to advance others.

Here are just a few examples from the Hadith and Islamic Law[184]:

Sahih Bukhari (52:269) - "The Prophet said, 'War is deceit.'" The context of this is thought to be the murder of Usayr ibn Zarim and his thirty unarmed men by Muhammad's men after he "guaranteed" them safe passage.

Sahih Bukhari (49:857) - "He who makes peace between the people by inventing good information or saying good things, is not a liar." Lying is permitted when the end justifies the means.

Islamic Law: Reliance of the Traveler (p. 746 - 8.2) "Speaking is a means to achieve objectives. If a praiseworthy aim is attainable through both telling the truth and lying, it is unlawful to accomplish through lying because there is no need for it. When it is possible to achieve such an aim by lying but not by telling the truth, it is permissible to lie if attaining the goal is permissible (i.e. when the purpose of lying is to circumvent someone who is preventing one from doing something permissible), and obligatory to lie if the goal is obligatory. . ..it is religiously precautionary in all cases to employ words that give a misleading impression. . .."

As the intent of "stealth jihad" is to "sabotage" a nation from within, it often camouflages itself in "moderation." Islamists take on the role of "moderate" Muslims who enjoin themselves to Sharia based organizations and subsequently present themselves as "moderates and servants" when negotiating differences within society. Yet, their community and home life are explicitly governed by Sharia law—Linda Sansour[185] is an excellent example of such. And since Sharia is a totalitarian system—it is imputed upon all aspects of civil society and human life, both public and private.

Regardless of how it is cloaked or uncloaked, Sharia law is anti-Constitutional. There is no rhetoric, dialogue, or government inclusion that can change the Sharia discourse. Why? Because Sharia fundamentally rejects democratic tenets which are the bedrock of American society and values. It rejects the rights of the governed to "'make law for themselves'; freedom of conscience as displayed through self-government and individual liberty; freedom of expression which includes the right to criticize sharia; economic liberty which includes the right to private property; equitable treatment for both male and female; freedom from cruel and harsh punishment, inclusive of the use of terrorism; and the use of 'mechanisms of federalism and democracy' to resolve political differences."[186]

The realization that there are Muslim organizations within America that seek to supplant the American Constitution through "stealth jihad" or "civilization jihad" cannot be ignored.

During the United States vs. Holy Land Foundation terrorist finance trial in 2008, the *Explanatory Memorandum on the General Strategic Goal for the Group*[187] was entered as evidence. The document was written in 1991 by Mohamed Akram, a senior Hamas leader in the U.S. and a member of the Board of Directors of the Muslim Brotherhood (MB) in North America. The MB is also known as the Ikhwan.

The term Ikhwan is important because the document clarifies that the Islamic Movement is "a Muslim Brotherhood effort, led by the Ikhwan in America."

Who are Ikhwans? Muslim Brotherhood ideologues such as Abu al-A'la Maududi, Hassan al-Banna, and Sayyid Qutb. They are known as "Ikhwan ideologues." They are those who have "recast modern jihad in the fiery language of revolution and anti-colonialism. . .. and not just strictly warfare to expand Islamic legal and political dominance."[188] All three have adopted a narrative that declares, *"the overthrow of unjust governments to be lawful."*[189]

Furthermore, Qutb, in his book *Milestones*, refers to the abolishment of all "satanic forces and satanic systems of life" as a reason for Jihad. According to Team B II, "satanic systems of life" means, "the way of life practiced in western-style liberal democracies—the way of the infidel, the Westerner, the non-Muslim." [190] Hence, Ikhwans are those enjoined to the Muslim Brotherhood who follow, practice, and execute the ideology of these three Ikhwan idealogues.[191]

A closer look at the Explanatory Memorandum reveals sits stealth jihad agenda:

Paragraph 1, §§1 and 2, Explanatory Memorandum, 18, reads:

The general strategic goal of the Group in America which was approved by the Shura Council and the Organizational Conference for the year [1987] is "Enablement of Islam in North America, meaning: establishing an effective and a stable Islamic Movement led by the Muslim Brotherhood which adopts Muslim' causes domestically and globally, and which works to expand the observant Muslim base, aims at unifying and directing Muslims' efforts, presents Islam as a civilization alternative, and supports the global Islamic State wherever it is."

Paragraph 4, of the Explanatory Memorandum, 20, describes the "Process of Settlement":

In order for Islam and its Movement to become "a part of the homeland" in which it lives, "stable" in its land, "rooted" in the spirits and minds of its people, "enabled" in the lives of its society and has firmly-established "organizations" on which the Islamic structure is built and with which the testimony of civilization is achieved, the Movement must plan and struggle to obtain, "the keys" and "the tools" of this process in carrying out this grand mission as a "Civilization Jihadist" responsibility which lies on the shoulders of Muslims and—on top of them—the Muslim Brotherhood in this country. Among these keys and tools are the following. . .."

Lastly, Paragraph 4, §4, of the Explanatory Memorandum refers to "Understanding the role of the Muslim Brotherhood in North America." It reads as follows:

The Process of settlement is a "Civilization-Jihadist Process" with all that the word means. The Ikhwan must understand that their work in the America is a kind of grand Jihad in eliminating and destroying Western Civilization from within and "sabotaging" its miserable house by their hands and the hands of believers so that it is eliminated and God's religion is made victorious over all other religions. . ..It is a

Muslim's destiny to perform Jihad and work wherever he is and wherever he lands until the final hour comes, and there is no escape from that destiny except for those who choose to slack."

This "Explanatory Memorandum" reflects Hamas' Charter Article 2:[192]

The Islamic Resistance Movement is the branch of the Muslim Brotherhood in Palestine. The Muslim Brotherhood is a global organization and the largest Islamic movement in modern times. It excels in profound understanding and has an exact, fully comprehensive perception of all Islamic concepts in all areas of life: understanding and thought, politics and economics, education and social affairs, law and government, spreading (i.e., indoctrinating the tenets of radical) Islam and teaching, art and the media, by that which is hidden and by martyrdom and in the other areas of life.

Article 6 of the Hamas Charter opens another caveat that was visible throughout the Obama administration: The progressive distancing of itself from Israel.

The Islamic Resistance Movement is uniquely Palestinian. It has faith in Allah and adopts Islam as its way of life. It acts to fly the banner of Allah over all of Palestine, because people of all religions can live in the shadow of Islam in tranquility and security for their lives, property, and rights. However, in the absence of Islam, a conflict develops that furthers injustice, corruption grows, more conflicts are created, and [eventually] war breaks out.

Although Jihad, external or internal, is present within the Muslim Brotherhood, it too was excised from the Obama Muslim doctrine and removed from its terrorist list. John Brennan, Obama's top counterterrorism advisor, insisted that President [Obama] did not believe there was a "global war" with Islamic terrorists. And because of such, Brennan announced that "the term 'jihadists' will no longer be used to describe our enemies."[193] He reserved the use of the term to describe al Qaeda's ruthless operatives. This lack of understanding as to the goal and connection of jihad to Sharia law and Islam's obligation to sabotage American democracy for the greater moral good, revealed two things: the effectiveness of the lobby of Islamic organizations[194] and the ease in which "stealth jihad" operated within the Obama administration.

For America, the question remains, how valuable is democracy and the individual freedoms it affords? Is it worth fighting for? If indeed the agenda of Islamist is to deceive America through stealth jihad, how can their agenda be exposed without infringing upon the rights or inflicting harm upon moderate American Muslims? How could the trend of Islamic appeasement be reversed within the Trump administration? And would it be in the best interest of democracy to call out "stealth jihad" and insist that the Islamists remove all anti-American rhetoric, process of settlement, civilization jihad, grand jihad, stealth jihad strategies, indoctrination of radical tenets, terrorism support, sedition and inclination to subvert the Constitution from their charters, training manuals, and organizational documents? With a new President, maybe it is time to restore American Democracy and the supremacy of its law rooted in the Constitution—so that all peoples continue to have the right to liberty, freedom, and the pursuit of happiness.

ॐ

The List

Following is a list of organizations associated with the Muslim Brotherhood:[195]

- Islamic Society of North America (ISNA)

- Muslim Student Association (MSA)

- Muslim Communities Association (MCA)

- Association of Muslim Social Scientists (AMSS)

- Association of Muslim Scientists and Engineers (AMSE)

- Islamic Medical Association (IMA)

- Islamic Teaching Center (ITC)

- North American Islamic Trust (NAIT)

- Foundation for International Development (FID)

- Islamic Housing Cooperative (IHC)

- Islamic Centers Division (ICD)

- American Trust Publications (ATP)

- Audio-Visual Center (AVC)

- Islamic Book Service (IBS)

- Muslim Businessmen Association (MBA)

- Muslim Youth of North America (MYNA)

- ISNA Fiqh Committee (IFC)

- ISNA Political Awareness Committee (IPAC)

- Islamic Education Department (IED)

- Muslim Arab Youth Association (MAYA)

- Malaysian (sic) Islamic Study Group (MISG)

- Islamic Association for Palestine (IAP)

- United Association for Studies and Research (UASR)

- Occupied Land Fund (OLF)

- Mercy International Association (MIA)

- Islamic Circle of North America (ICNA)

- Baitul Mal Inc (BMI)

- International Institute for Islamic Thought (IIIT)

- Islamic Information Center (IIC)

Several of the preeminent Muslim-American organizations in the United States today (notably, the Council on American-Islamic Relations [CAIR], the Muslim Public Affairs Council [MPAC] and the Islamic Free Market Institute [II]) were not established in 1991 when this document was adopted by the Muslim Brotherhood.

To be considered by the Muslim Brotherhood to be one of "our organizations" or an "organization of our friends," each of these entities had to embrace the Ikhwan creed: "Allah is our goal; the Messenger is our guide: the Qur'an is our law; Jihad is our means; and martyrdom in the way of Allah is our inspiration."

ℰ◌

CHAPTER NINE

The Israel Shift

". . .there will I deal with and execute judgment upon them for the treatment of My people and My heritage Israel, whom they have scattered among the nations and because they have divided My land." Joel 3:2

∞

O n September 20th, 2016 President Obama addressed the United Nations General Assembly. In his farewell address, Obama compromised America's loyalty to the nation of Israel by saying that Israel must recognize that it *cannot* "permanently occupy Palestinian land." However, the compromise pales against the reality that Obama orchestrated the December 23, 2016, UN Security Council Resolution 2334.[196]

Now, to be fair, Obama went on to say that the Palestinians must also "reject incitement and recognize Israel's legitimacy." Yet, there is a huge gap on the Truth

O Meter between these two demands. First, the Palestinians are a non-state actor. They are not a nation, a legitimate state, nor a recognized partner for peace. World leaders want to legitimize them, but thus far the Palestinians have rejected all proposals and Israel's right to exist—for this reason they do not have a state.

Hence, for World leaders and global institutions to blame Israel is very telling and it smells of a reminiscent ideology that brought Hitler to power. The European Union, United Nations, and the former President lived in a make-believe world ignoring the reality on the ground— the Palestinians are occupying Israel's land, not the other way around. On the flip side, Israel doesn't see the Palestinians as occupiers. They are welcome under Israel's umbrella of sovereignty—unless they commit acts of terrorism.

With that said, I would like to share an insight rarely mentioned regarding the two-state-solution—the choice of the Palestinian people.

As we discussed in the last two chapters, the Muslim Brotherhood has an agenda to replace the U.S. Constitution with Sharia Law or at the very least, use the Constitution to impose Sharia Law upon the American Muslim society. For many democratically inclined Muslims, that is a horrifying thought. And so, it is, for many Palestinians who live under the democratic rule of Israel.

During my many discussions with young Palestinian women, unanimously they have told me that they do not want to be under the control of Hamas, the militant wing of the Muslim Brotherhood, or any Sharia-based government. They would prefer to remain under the autonomy of Israel. For many young Palestinians the whole Islam initiative is a real turn off. They don't want to be forced to pray, yet they want to pray. They don't want to be compelled to wear burqas, niqabs or hijabs. Instead, they desire to choose their religious involvement, integrate in to Israeli society, attend college, become professionals, have careers, start families and live the semblance of a more democratic and free life.

For this reason, alone, we must find another solution than the old, out-of-date, and unwanted two-state solution. Putting the Palestinian people under the bondage and oppression of Sharia Law by agreeing to a two-state solution—is not upholding human rights, a just Middle East democracy or religious freedom.

Of course, there is also the issue of the West Bank— the biblical land of Judea and Samaria—Israeli territory that the European Union and United Nations want to give to the Palestinian Authority. Strategically, this makes the two-state solution a death trap for Israel. Let me explain why:

First, towards the end of the Obama era, the Palestinian Authority (PA) was losing political ground and the resignation of President Mahmoud Abbas was looming.[197] The implications of such could increase the influence of Hamas, the terrorist organization that controls Gaza—begging the question, "if the West Bank is given over to the Palestinians, and the PA disbanded, would it naturally fall into the hands of Hamas and the Al-Quds Brigades?"

Well, since President Trump took office, a concerted effort began within his administration to bring peace to the Middle East.

Abbas did a 180. He came out of the shadows of near retirement to ensure point in the peace negotiations. He was given the taunting job of reigning in Hamas and creating a unity government. To accomplish a reconciliatory vision, Abbas put the squeeze on Gaza—reducing both electric and water supply rations due to bills that were in arrears. His tactic was intended to: 1) cause Hamas to surrender control over Gaza and 2) demonize Israel by making it appear that it was Israel who was callously withholding aid to Gaza.

On November 1, 2017 Hamas handed over five border crossings to the Palestinian Authority (PA), also known as Fatah. The handover, brokered by Egypt, was part of a signed agreement to restore the status quo in Gaza after the 2007 split between the PA and Hamas. It is believed that this initial step, with more to come will result in a better quality of life for the Gazan citizens.[198]

As beautiful as it appears on the surface, a unity government between Hamas and the PA conjures up deep concerns as to the ultimate end game of Mahmoud Abbas; who, after the announcement of the U.S. Embassy move, went rogue. Consider the fact that Mahmoud Abbas is a "foreign leader who harbors or supports terrorism."[199] Yes, he controls the Al Aqsa Martyrs' Brigade[200], a division of Fatah and a terrorist organization on the U.S terror list. And, if you ponder the fact that Abbas was grooming a terrorist in prison to replace him then it is easy to see that the absence of a Hamas controlled Gaza does not equate with the absence of terror. On the contrary, Hamas continues to align itself with the Iran and it's growing axis in the region. And, as a show of spite towards the U.S., just days before Abbas met President Trump at the White House, the Al Aqsa Martyrs' Brigade staged a public rally in full regalia firing weapons. Furthermore, the PA continues to fund terrorists and their family members. And if this is the reality of a what is touted as a "partner for peace" without state status, what do you think will unfold if Abbas and the PA negotiated state status?

In addition to the PA conundrum, to consider the challenges of Israel's National Security we must look at the whole picture: Hamas in Gaza, the Al Aqsa Martyrs' Brigade spread out in Palestinian communities, the terrorist group Al-Quds in the West Bank, Hezbollah is Iran's proxy parked along the Lebanese border and now in the Lebanese government, and Iran is building a land bridge from Tehran to Beirut, while ISIS gathers along the Egyptian border. Under a two-state solution this scenario would be heightened tenfold. And with the Obama infused funds of the U.S. government,[201] Iran's funding of terrorist organizations such as Hamas, Hezbollah, and Islamic Jihad[202] has never been more volatile.

On August 15th, Deborah Danan, wrote an excellent article for Breitbart entitled, *Hezbollah, Hamas Officials Confirm: Iran Funds Our Activity*. She quotes Nasrallah, the Secretary General of Hezbollah while speaking to Lebanon's Al Ahed news (translated by the Middle East Media Research Institute (MEMRI). He clarified Hezbollah's budget source:

> Hezbollah's budget—its salaries and expenditures, its food and drink, weapons and missiles—[all come from] Iran. Is that clear?. . ..As long as Iran has money we have money. Do you require greater transparency than that[?] The funds earmarked for us do not reach us through the banks. We receive them the same way we receive our missiles with which we threaten Israel.

Her article further captures Iran's funding of Hamas. Abu Marzouq, deputy head of Hamas's political bureau, tweeted on June 15, "The aid extended by Iran to the Palestinian resistance in provisions, training, and funds are not comparable [to any other aid], and most other countries cannot match it." Also, former Lebanese minister and known supporter of Hezbollah Wiam

Wahhab tweeted, "Iran funded resistance in Palestine to restore Jerusalem, Al-Aqsa, and the Church of the Sepulcher." Note that the funding is not to build an infrastructure for the Palestinian people, but for terrorism.

Lastly, I would like to mention the terrorist group Palestinian Islamic Jihad (PIJ) whose militant wing is called Al-Quds Brigades.[203] This organization operates out of the West Bank, with its strongholds located primarily in Hebron and Jenin.[204] Along with Hamas, Al-Quds formed as an offshoot of the Muslim Brotherhood. And, they too are funded by Iran. Danan writes:

> Iran also restored aid to the Gaza-based Islamic Jihad after suspending its aid to the terror group following disagreements concerning the crisis in Yemen. *Al-Sharq Al-Awsat* reported that an Islamic Jihad delegation headed by secretary-general Ramadan Shalah visited Iran in April 2016; during this visit, Tehran renewed its sponsorship of the organization after the latter accepted its terms.

The above is just a taste of numerous articles and speeches that cite Iran's involvement in supporting terrorism against Israel. But the real issue is that these terrorist organizations have only one agenda—to delegitimize Israel and wipe Israel off the map. For this reason, alone, it would be foolish to reward terrorists with a state. A two-state solution is not just rewarding terrorism, but it is sanctioning their anti-Israel agenda.

જી

Gush Katif

Do you remember Gush Katif? A beautiful, cultivated bloc of seventeen Jewish communities located in Southern Gaza. These communities were the buffer zone between Egypt and Gaza. It was the summer of 2005 when the IDF forcibly removed the remaining citizens of these communities from their homes. Ten thousand plus Israeli citizens turned over their homes, businesses, educational facilities and operational plants to the Palestinian Authority as a gesture of peace; only to watch them destroyed. What did Israel get in return? A Hamas terrorist base and training camp that, in 2014, launched over 4,000 missiles into Israel.

Gush Katif was nothing but a futile exercise in self-delusion among World leaders; a callisthenic in appeasement led by the U.S. State Department.[205] One terrorist base and training camp is more than enough. To turn a blind eye to the reality that Hamas would turn the West Bank into a second terrorist base is to be an accomplice to mass murder and Israel's potential annihilation.

But, there are other productive solutions and opportunities especially through education, social media, women, and youth that produce steps towards a path to peace than a two-state solution.

The narrative purported by the United Nations and anti-Israel NGO's is making the world believe that Israel illegally occupies the West Bank. This is a lie, a dangerously deceptive lie, that leads us back to Obama's second statement during his final U.N. address.

The second statement Obama made was correct; Israel is a legitimate nation with borders. Israel's borders, which include the West Bank (Judea and ancient Shomron) were purchased with Israeli blood, sweat, and tears in 1967 after five Arab nations presumptuously attacked Israel with the intent to destroy her. In fact, in Sunday's Jerusalem Post (September 25, 2016), Oded Revivi wrote an excellent commentary entitled, *Mr. President: The Israeli settlements are legal.* Concerning the legality of 1967 borders, he said:

> The State of Israel captured territory that did not belong to any other country and which was already designated for the establishment of the Jewish State. The legal status of Palestine, which the Balfour Declaration (1917) earmarked as the future "national home for the Jewish people," was determined by the League of Nations (1920), the San Remo agreements (1920) and the British Mandate, in addition to being approved by the US Congress (1922). In the absence of any other laws, these laws still apply today, making Israel's presence legal and valid.

Obama's narrative that Israel is a legitimate nation that cannot occupy the land of an illegitimate nation permanently is equivalent to calling evil good and good evil. Once again, Obama sided with illegal, misguiding Americans regarding its faithful ally Israel.

Wherever you stand on the two-state solution, President Trump and his administration have worked to reverse anti-Israel bias, restore faithful relations, consider new paths to peace, and do the unthinkable, move of the U.S. Embassy from Tel Aviv to Jerusalem. So, let's go there!

෨

Next Year in Jerusalem?

In 1967, Israel won a war waged against her by Egypt, Jordan and Syria—in 6 days. That's why the 1967 war is known as the "miraculous 6 Day War." Israel's victory over a surprise attack by Egyptian, Jordanian and Syrian forces ensured her legal acquisition of the Golan Heights, Gaza, the Sinai Peninsula and Transjordan (the present day 'West Bank' aka, Judea and Samaria).

What's important for you to know is, at that time, the Hashemite Kingdom of Jordan was controlling the West Bank (Transjordan), which included East Jerusalem—not the Palestinians. Think about it—Israel gained territory from Jordan not the Palestinians. Therefore, the whole narrative (you've been hearing for decades) that Israel has been building settlements in "Palestinian occupied territory since 1967" is fraudulent. For the Palestinians to cry wolf against Israel for their disenfranchisement (perpetuated by their own leaders) is not only a revision of history but, also, misplaced anger. The reality is that they were betrayed by the very nation that adopted them, Jordan.

By the way, did you know that the Transjordan region is in the Hebrew Scriptures, Septuagint, and subsequent Bible versions? Yes! It describes the territory settled by the tribes of Rueben, Gad and the half tribe of Manasseh.[206]

And with all the concrete present and past evidence that Israel has both the legal right to, and the lawful habitation of the West Bank (modern day Judea and Samaria) including Jerusalem, the International community has done everything, apart from committing another Holocaust, to punish Israel.

The U.N.'s obsession with anti-Israel resolutions and rhetoric is palpable. The game changer? Jerusalem. Once Jerusalem came under Israeli sovereignty the International community went crazy. Since 1967, the U.N., inclusive of all its divisions, has condemned Israel approximately, if not more than, 400 times.[207] In fact, resolution 2334 began with a reaffirmation of every major resolution against Jerusalem and the so called "settlements" since 1967:

Reaffirming its relevant resolutions, including resolutions 242 (1967), 338 (1973), 446 (1979), 452 (1979), 465 (1980), 476 (1980), 478 (1980), 1397 (2002), 1515 (2003), and 1850 (2008).

Of resolution 2334, Alan Dershowitz, who voted for Obama, said:

I think President Trump's decision to recognize Jerusalem as the capital of Israel is the perfect response to President Obama's outrageous orchestration of the Security Council resolution which he pushed through as a lame duck, that declared the Western Wall to be illegally occupied territory, the Hebrew University, Hadassah Hospital, the Jewish Quarter - according to this resolution that was basically pushed through by Obama, these are outrageously flagrant violations of international law. . ..You say it's occupied, we say it's the capital.[208]

Now, here we are, over a year since resolution 2334, with a decisive date to move the U.S. Embassy—May 14, 2018. Wow! Can you imagine? Exactly 70 years after Ben Gurion declared Israel a State!

Have you read the *Declaration of the Establishment of the State of Israe?l*[209] You should. Here's a snippet:

Accordingly we, members of the People's Council, Representatives of the Jewish Community of Eretz-Israel and of the Zionist Movement, are here assembled on the day of the termination of the British Mandate over Eretz-Israel and, by virtue of the British Mandate over Eretz-Israel and, by virtue of our natural and historic right and on the strength of the resolution of the United Nations General Assembly, hereby declare the establishment of a Jewish State in Eretz-Israel, to be known as the State of Israel.

On May 14, 2018 another speech will be written in the analogs of Israel's history, a *Declaration of Jerusalem as the Capital of Israel.*

A testament to the faithfulness of G-D, the truth of His Word, and the hope of His soon coming redemption! Zechariah said it this way, "And the LORD shall inherit Judah his portion in the holy land and shall choose Jerusalem again. Be silent, O all flesh, before the LORD: for he is raised up out of his holy habitation."[210]

This shift of the Embassy from Tel Aviv to Jerusalem is no small matter. In fact, it will send shock waves around the world. The potential of war immediately thereafter is very great, if indeed the Arab world and its partners follow suit to the 1948-49 war.

It will awaken two kingdoms for a final showdown: G-D's and Satan's. Now, you may not believe in all that stuff, and that's ok. However, you cannot deny the fierce battle surrounding the Israeli-Arab conflict, and that a move of such significance will only fuel that struggle. It's also hard to reject the reality that there is something markedly unique when it comes to Israel and its capital Jerusalem.

Furthermore, Jerusalem is central to all "end of day" or "in that day" verses of Scripture. In fact, the entire book of Zechariah concerns itself with Jerusalem, in the last days. Consider Isaiah's words, "And give him (G-D) no rest, till he establish and till he make Jerusalem a praise in the earth."[211] Or King David's who cried out, "If I forget thee, O Jerusalem, let my right hand forget her cunning."[212] And prolifically wrote, "the LORD does build up Jerusalem: he gathers together the outcasts of Israel."[213] Yes, Jerusalem's restoration holds incredible significance, don't you think?

The shift of the U.S. Embassy will also solidify the divide of nations and organizations who are either "for or against" Israel. Soon thereafter, nation after nation will move its Embassy to Jerusalem. According to Scripture, when the Messiah reigns Israel will be the capital of the world—how close are we to that end? I don't know, but what I do know is the shift has begun—and no man, nation, or resolution can stop it now.

෴

Saudi Arabia

Before we leave this chapter, let's talk about Saudi Arabia—another chess piece in the status of Jerusalem, the Temple Mount and the Embassy move.

Since the first meeting in Riyadh with the Trump Team (Jared Kushner and Jason Greenblatt) to further Middle East Peace between Israel, the Palestinians and the Arab world, the Saudi government has stepped out of the shadows as a U.S. ally and mediator between the Israeli and Palestinian peace agreement.

The recent actions of the Saudi heir, Crown Prince Mohammed bin Salman is shaking both the ME region and Saudi Arabia itself! Reports of new laws allowing women to drive and the arrests of Saudi's political elites on corruption charges are flowing from Arab media outlets. And on behalf of the U.S., Saudi has forced the resignation of Lebanese Prime Minister Hariri and given an ultimatum to Palestinian Authority President Abbas— accept Trump's plan or resign in anticipation of a peace deal that would be agreed upon by Israel, the Palestinians and even the Sunni Shia Muslim world.

Now all of that, especially in light of the Qatar crisis, has technically backfired when it comes to Abbas. However, the emergence of the Saudi's on the world stage is prolific. Few realize that the Saudi's are ancient Sheba and Dedan. And, according to the book of Ezekiel chapter 38, Sheba and Dedan, along with other Arab elites and youth, will play a very decisive mediatory role when the Arab world and the nations come up against the Land and Jerusalem.

However, the immediate highlight worth sharing is the Crown Prince Salman's *Saudi Arabia Vision 2030*.[214] In an interview with Al Arabiya TV, the Prince confirmed that an IPO[215]of approximately 5% of Aramco stock, Saudi's largest oil company, will be released. He also highlighted the following three pillars:

- First pillar is our status as the heart of the Arab and Islamic worlds.
- Second pillar is our determination to become a global investment powerhouse
- Third pillar is transforming our unique strategic location into a global hub connecting three continents, Asia, Europe and Africa.

With *Vision 2030,* Saudi Arabia is poised to lead the Arab world toward westernization and modernization. Amazing, when you think that Ezekiel foresaw this 2500 years ago![216]

Stay tuned—global events surrounding Israel are about to get real exciting!

೮౨

CHAPTER TEN

Foreign Policy

"You shall not pervert judgment; you shall not respect persons (or foreign leaders), neither take a gift: for a gift (bribe) does blind the eyes of the wise, and pervert the words of the righteous." Deuteronomy 16:19

⁊ↄ

H ave you seen the movie Thirteen Hours? It is the true story of the terrorist attack on the United States consulate and CIA outpost in Benghazi. It speaks volumes of the failed foreign policy of the Obama administration and the Clinton State Department. You cannot watch the movie and not wonder, "why?" Hearing the words, "I called for air cover, they never came" near the end of the movie, leaves you numb and enraged over the intentional negligence of the United States Government. How could our government let this happen?

Few realize that we had soldiers being killed in Afghanistan, not because of terrorism or sniper fire, but because our military did not receive clearance, weapons, and assets needed to fight—the result of an administration selling out America. Let's just take a glimpse at what failed foreign policy looks like.

Hillary Clinton served as Secretary of State from 2009 - 2013. In just five years, she left in her wake a death toll that is estimated between 700,000 to 2 million.[217] The failed foreign policy under her watch has resulted in Russian expansionism, China's Nine-Dash line, the rise and expansion of ISIL, the Syrian Refugee crimes and crisis, and Iran's terror trifecta.

To understand why, let's go back to 2008, just before both President Obama and Secretary of State Clinton stepped on the scene.

While Obama campaigned on improving Russian relations in 2008, few realized what this meant for the Eastern Block of Europe—countries under Soviet control during the Cold War. When Russia invaded Georgia in 2008, the United States stepped in immediately by deploying U.S. warships into the Black Sea and recalling Georgia troops from Iraq. President Bush also froze bilateral relations with Russia. He then went one step further to protect the Eastern Block with plans to build installations that housed missile defense interceptors of which Poland and the Czech Republic agreed to host.

After Hillary's appointment as Secretary of State, her first assignment was to follow through on Obama's vision for Russian revival. Hence, in March 2009 she met with Russian Foreign Minister Sergei Lavrov. Six months later the U.S. canceled the deployment of the interceptors to Poland and the Czech Republic; leaving them without the economic or security benefits we promised.

Let's bring this down to a personal level. Have you ever been betrayed by a friend for personal gain? This type of thing often happens in high school when girlfriends steal boyfriends and vice versa. It also happens when opportunity knocks to climb the corporate ladder, or when family members come into an inheritance. Amazing how quickly one can betray another when personal gain is involved. I am not saying you would—and hopefully, your character is better than that, but none of us are exempt from its temptation. Whether you have, or you haven't—our government has and neither Poland nor the Czech Republic have forgotten.

Russia's Vladimir Putin on the other hand, immediately perceived this buttering up to Russia and subsequent concessions for what it was—American betrayal. Notably, he had already given Poland and the Czech Republic a tongue lashing for siding with America, and now that they were humiliated by the World's Sovereign, Putin's expansionist agenda could move forward—Crimea, Middle East, Georgia and the Ukraine.

With the only superpower holding Russia in check bought with a bribe, who would now keep Russia in check?

Jonathan Levin writes in his article, *Hillary Clinton's Foreign Policy Failures,* that this was "the first of what would become a pattern, the U.S. sacrificed allies' interests to a rival in the fatuous hope that the rival would feel some sort of gratitude or obligation in return." Has that happened? Does Russia feel a "sort of gratitude" or obligation to America and her interest? I say not.

The night of the third debate between Trump and Clinton, I was sitting in a hospital family lounge waiting to return to a dear friend's room. The TV was on and I just happened to catch the Clinton Trump exchange over the Russian hacks. From my perspective, it was Clinton's attempt to make Trump a scapegoat for the hacked emails uploaded by WikiLeaks. She was also pointing the finger at him for Russian espionage, and for being a close buddy of Vladimir Putin—like this was a horrible thing. My mouth opened, and the all too familiar words blurted out, "what a liar." You see, I had just finished researching a generous amount of material on Clinton and Russia, of which the above only scrapped the surface. You know that's what guilty people do, they make others take the blame.

On a side note, have you asked yourself why Russia would hack Hillary, Podesta, Soros, the State Department, etc.? Well, not because of Trump, I assure you. Remember the Panama Paper Scandal in chapter one? There is your answer. This is the group who went after Putin and Russia's just returning the deed—giving them a little taste of their own medicine, wouldn't you say? Now back to Clinton and Trump.

Do you remember the cookie jar on the kitchen counter? The one your mother said, "don't touch?" Well, I loved the cookie jar growing up. I would sneak a few cookies and then cover up my naughty escapade by rearranging the cookies in the cookie jar, so it looked fuller. One day, my mother noticed that almost all the cookies were gone and called all of us kids to the kitchen. She lined us up and asked, "who ate the cookies?" We all shook our heads "no." "No one ate the cookies?" mom asked raising her voice. "Nope," we all muttered under our breaths. Finally, I spoke up and blamed my brother. "Yep," my brother did it. He got a spanking, and I felt horrible that he took the punishment for my cookie sins. I am not sure if I ever confessed, but I did stop making my brother the scapegoat for my hand in the cookie jar. The connection?

Trump was Hillary's scapegoat for her folly with Russia, and the media just played along.

Do you remember the Uranium One deal? It was another deal brokered behind the scenes under the guise of the "Russian reset" giving Russia 20% in U.S. Uranium assets.

In May 2016, Peter Schweizer, author of Clinton Cash, wrote in his article, *One Year of Silence on Hillary Clinton Uranium Deal*[218] the following:

> Things got worse for the Clintons a few days later when two *New York Times* Pulitzer Prize-winning investigative reporters, Jo Becker and Mike McIntire, took two of the most explosive chapters in the book and did their own digging. What they found confirmed what I had reported. They ran a 3,000-word, front-page article in the paper confirming that: Bill and Hillary Clinton had helped a Canadian financier named Frank Giustra, and a small Canadian company obtain a lucrative uranium mining concession from the dictator in Kazakhstan; The same Canadian company, renamed Uranium One, bought uranium concessions in the United States; The Russian government came calling and sought to buy that Canadian company for a price that would mean big profits for the Canadian investors; For the Russians to buy that Canadian company, it would require the approval of the Obama administration, including Hillary's State Department, because uranium is a strategically important commodity; Nine shareholders in Uranium One just happened to provide more than $145 million in donations to the Clinton Foundation in the run-up to State Department approval; Some of the donations, including those from the Chairman of Uranium One, Ian Teler, were kept secret, even though the Clintons

promised to disclose all donations; Hillary's State Department approved the deal; The Russian government now owns 20 percent of U.S. uranium assets.

In short, here was what you might call a radioactive scandal. It included secret donations, the Russian government, foreign financiers, more than $145 million, and Bill and Hillary Clinton. Funny, it's all just emerging in 2018 because of the Mueller probe—however, the question still remains, "why hasn't Clinton been indicted?"

Concerning Clinton's bribery, RealClearPolitics wrote,

If foreign governments, including adversarial ones like Russia, paid the Clinton Foundation huge sums of money, they assured themselves favorable treatment. (Mr. Clinton received $500,000 for a Moscow speech from a Russian investment bank with links to the Kremlin that was pursuing the purchase of Uranium One, a uranium mining company.)[219]

And then there was the post-agreement interview with Rosatom's chief executive, Sergei Kiriyenko, who told Putin, "Few could have imagined in the past that we would own 20 percent of U.S. reserves."[220]

Rosatom is Russia's atomic energy corporation. It has regional centers in Western, Central and Eastern Europe, Latin America, Central Asia, East and South-East Asia, the Middle East and North Africa.[221] The India Times reported the following:

> According to South Asia CEO Alexey Pimenov, the worldwide creation of a regional center's network was due to the expansion of Rosatom's global presence and a long-term development strategy, according to which the purpose of the company for the next ten years was to increase the portfolio of foreign orders up to $150 billion. Recently, Rosatom opened a regional center in Mumbai India.[222]

So, while the end of the Cold War was supposed to bring Nuclear Arms depreciation between the U.S. and Russia, and while the Obama administration was actively depreciating our U.S. Nuclear Arms capabilities to create a safer non-nuclear world, Russia was busy building its nuclear presence throughout the world. Oh, and I don't want to forget that Iran is too! But then again, we should have expected such because we were leading from behind. Yes, and all the while, the Clinton's seemed to be at the top of the Hill in the nuclear business.

Lastly, when it comes to bribes, the kind of bribes that blind judgment, check this report out:

> More than half, to be exact at least 85 of 154 people from private interests who met or had phone conversations scheduled with Clinton while she led the State Department donated to her family charity or pledged commitments to its international programs,

according to a review of State Department calendars released so far to The Associated Press. Combined, the 85 donors contributed as much as $156 million. At least 40 donated more than $100,000 each, and 20 gave more than $1 million.[223]

Those are staggering numbers that cannot be ignored. The question one must ask after reading the documented depth of bribery is, "what will America's future hold if the American people willingly ignore truth?"

Let's move on to the Asian pivot—Russia's there too!

৪০

Asian Pivot

The 2011 Asian shift is known as the "pivot" in American foreign policy. This pivot from the Middle East to Asia is referred to as the "Potemkin pivot." Have you ever heard the word "Potemkin?" Well here it is, a new Scrabble word.

Potemkin means, "having a false or deceptive appearance, especially one presented for, the purpose of propaganda."[224] It also has the connotation of fraudulent or counterfeit. The term came from the surname of a Russian soldier named Grigori Aleksandrovich (1739-91). He was the lover of Empress Catherine II. To impress her into believing Crimea was a rich country, he built a fake village known as the Potemkin village along the banks of the Dnieper River. Hence, the "Potemkin pivot" in foreign policy exists, "solely to impress."

Those who understand the shift of the previous Obama administration from the Middle East to Asia will quickly point out that Clinton was center stage in this shift; and that there is no propaganda that can redeem the domino effect of the destruction it triggered. Without question, the "pivot" which later became known as the "Rebalance of Asia" has enhanced U.S. presence in Asia—one which was severely lacking. The most notable outgrowth of America's presence was the Trans-Pacific Partnership (TPP), an agreement among 12 nations representing nearly 40 percent of global GDP. This agreement was vehemently contested by both Donald Trump and Bernie Sanders. And after President Trump took office it was abandoned.[225] Let's look at just a few reasons why.

The first reason, which holds true for the Iranian Nuclear Deal as well, was its secrecy. For the most part, all the negotiations of the TPP were done in secret, and the American public was not made aware of the agreement's contents. According to truthout.org, intellectual property concerns surrounding the deal and the TPP cannot be reversed or amended without the ratification of all 12 members. On July 8, 2016, Deena Zaidi, author for *Truthout* wrote:

> While the TPP benefits are mentioned broadly on the website, a leaked classified document posted by

WikiLeaks highlights intellectual property concerns. It observes that under the TPP deal, foreign firms will be allowed to "sue" governments for "unlimited compensation." Such arrangements could raise environmental and legal issues, leading to a conflict between domestic and international interests. Moreover, once adopted, TPP cannot be reversed or amended without the approval of all of its 12-member nations.[226]

Secondly, the TPP would benefit multinational corporations while further diminishing the American workforce. This trend was notable when one examined the lobbying expenditures for those in favor of the TPP. And thirdly, there were serious environmental concerns. The TPP received over 500 anti-TPP petitions from environmental groups that stated:

> The TPP and [Transatlantic Trade and Investment Partnership] would more than double the number of fossil fuel corporations that could follow TransCanada's example and challenge U.S. policies in private tribunals.[227]

Lastly, and most importantly was its threat to America's domestic policy. According to *Truthout*, former President Obama stated that the Trans-Pacific Partnership would benefit, "farmers, ranchers, and manufacturers by eliminating more than 18,000 taxes that various countries put on our products." Well, we have seen how well that benefit worked out between the European Union and the United Kingdom—they're still reeling from BREXIT.

Bernie Sanders also noted that the TPP "follows failed trade deals with Mexico, China and other low-wage countries that have cost millions of jobs and shut down tens of thousands of factories across the United States." And he is correct.

Failed trade deals like NAFTA have exploited foreign workers with uncensored child labor, low wages, and merciless working conditions. They've also put hundreds of thousands of Americans out of work.

An assessment of the TPP economic impact made by the U.S. International Trade Commission (ITC) concluded that that the TPP is likely to "have only a small positive effect on U.S. growth." And according to the Public Citizen, the Commission's "faulty methodologies led to overtly optimistic projections." These optimistic projections play out to a projected U.S. global trade deficit of $21.7 billion by 2032. The ITC believed that the deal is likely to "worsen the trade balances of 65 percent of 55 U.S. agriculture, manufacturing and services sectors." Lori Wallach, director of the Public Citizen's Global Trade Watch, stated that the ITC analysis "suggests that if ever implemented, the TPP could really be disastrous."[228]

And even though Clinton was fundamentally opposed to the TPP, she was the impetus behind the agreement. Hear what she said:

This agreement is not just about eliminating barriers to trade, although that is crucial for boosting U.S. exports and creating jobs here at home. It's also about agreeing on the rules of the road for an integrated Pacific economy that is open, free, transparent and fair. It will put in place strong protections for workers, the environment, intellectual property and innovation—all key American values.

For an agreement that had the potential to collapse the American domestic market to go as far as being approved by the 12 nations before awaiting ratification by Congress, there was unquestioningly another agenda, one which fit nicely into our chapter on borders.

There is much more that can be written about the Asian pivot; so, let me sum up its success and failure under the Obama administration in this manner, we made great inroads in building relations with our Asian partners, all except one. The one which appears to be the reason we made the pivot in the first place, China.

Clinton's vision for the Rebalance was a comprehensive policy joining diplomatic, military and economic engagement—all of which had the expressed goal of deterring Chinese expansion. And yet, due to sequestration of our military, we failed to achieve any actionable deterrence in the South China Sea. In fact, China continues to expand and encroach upon land and maritime boundaries of our allies.

ℰℴ

China's Nine-Dash Line

China has laid claim to approximately 85% of the maritime boundaries of the South China Sea (SCS), existing since 1947, in accordance to the China Nine-Dash Line.[229] The precise coordinates of the nine-dash-line boundaries China claims are not yet public. What was apparent though, is that while China was land grabbing new islands and laying claim to the territorial waters of our allies like the Philippines, President Obama's relationship with China's President Xi Jinping was deteriorating.

The reason for the decline appeared to originate from Obama's dismissal of his "red line" threat in Syria; even after evidence revealed that the Bashar Assad regime was gassing its people. Since that time, Xi Jinping knew he could defy the U.S. government and face no consequences.

To underscore his contempt for Obama, at the 2016 G-20 meeting, Xi Jinping "did not extend red-carpet stairs by which Obama could exit the plane after Air Force One landed at Hangzhou."[230] In contrast, Trump's November 2017 visit to China was welcomed. Not only did Trump receive the red-carpet stairs, but also a rare official dinner in the Forbidden City—never before has a U.S. President received such an honor.[231]

To emphasize how upside down our relationship with China had become, during the G-20 "Chinese boats were spotted at Scarborough Shoal, another waterway claimed by the Philippines where the U.S. has warned China not to stake out more artificial islands"[232] and the blatant affront to the U.S. was not even addressed.

According to the article, *Obama's Pivot Fails to Deter China*, Eli Lake writes,

> Obama's administration has in the last week encouraged the Philippines to work out the dispute over artificial islands with China on its own, despite the White House support for a ruling at The Hague in July against China's claims to the waterways it had claimed.[233]

Here again, the contrast between the Obama-Clinton Asian Pivot and Trump's 2017 Asian revival is staggering. The same Mr. Xi who defied Obama, honored Trump and notably, reigned in any signs of Chinese aggression in the SCS—even if it was only a token gesture.

As I bring this section on the Asian Pivot to a close, let's pause to reflect on another pattern that was present in the Obama administration—abandoning your allies and leaving them to fend for themselves; which I pointed out regarding Egypt. Obama had a way of getting nations entangled in domestic and foreign disputes and then, instead of leading them through the conflict, he put the onus of negotiating the outcome upon them. Consider the following:

While sitting in briefings at NATO I heard the words, "President Obama wants us to take more responsibility," after his Russian reset became Russian expansionism. While sitting in a class on the Arab Spring I heard the words, "where is America?" after President Obama's Middle East meddling brought down Mubarak in Egypt. After Clinton failed to renegotiate the Status of Forces agreement (SOFA)[234] needed for the U.S. to continue military support in Iraq, I heard the words, "the U.S. will train the elite Iraqi force to fight ISIS;"[235] as ISIS was growing. And after the death of Muammar Gaddafi, we ensured the Libyan nation, "we will help you build a democracy"—only to turn it over to radical insurgents resulting in a civil war. According to U.S. Army General Paul Vallely, "It was Obama and the State Department that created the weapon sale over there, basically arming the Muslim Brotherhood, backed Al-Qaeda radical Islamic elements over there—that created the problem in the first place.[236]"

The Arab Spring, sprung by Obama, is now the Arab Winter. After reviewing the links and connections between Obama, Clinton, their Muslim Brotherhood aides, and White House staff members in conjunction with the Arab Spring, there appeared to be a grander U.S.-Muslim Brotherhood strategy. The whole ordeal may have been a futile attempt for Obama to help organize a rise of the

Muslim Brotherhood in the Middle East. It failed. And in Egypt, home to the Muslim Brotherhood, it failed miserably—the Muslim Brotherhood was banished from the country. Did you know that Egypt felt so betrayed by the United States that it started purchasing its military arms from Russia? That is until Trump took office.

And when Obama's muddled plan for deterrence failed with China, he left our allies to fend for themselves. The outcome of the Obama-Clinton Asian pivot was tenuousness, at the very most. For Trump, it's been a foreign policy nightmare. Few make the connection between North Korea's nuclear threat and Obama's failed Asian Pivot, which played an eminent role in China's ineffective intervention on behalf of the North Korean crisis.

God forbid if Trump's administration is unable to thwart China's aggression against our allies or a North Korean nuke—all of which the jury's still out.

Of the Asian pivot, *five-thirty-eight* sums it up this way:

> In addition to economic considerations, these strategic concerns are a primary reason why, as Obama put it in his November 2011 speech before the Australian Parliament, "the United States will play a larger and long-term role in shaping this region and its future."[237]

On the security front, despite headlines over the past few years dominated by Russian adventurism in Ukraine, Iran's nuclear program and the rise of the Islamic State group, it is China—a rapidly rising power seeking to carve out a global leadership role for itself— that poses a challenge to both U.S. military preeminence and global leadership. China's large-scale land reclamation and aggressive patrolling in disputed waters in the South China Sea, in particular, have sparked concerns about Beijing's desire to reshape the Asia-Pacific region to suit its needs better.[238]

After Trump was elected he took a call from the Taiwan President Tsailng-wen. After congratulating him, they discussed strengthening U.S.-Taiwan relations. The State Department was furious, among others. Why? Because Trump stepped on another cockatrice egg. One that began under the Nixon administration in 1979 when we dumped Taiwan for China.

Well, now that you have a general idea about the China Nine-Dash Line, let me ask you, "Do you think Donald Trump was out of line when he spoke to the Taiwanese President or was he getting America back in line to protect our allies?" One call and the China Nine-Dash Line may have just lost a few dashes.

෴

The Sum of it All

So, let's reflect on a few events that transpired during the last four years of the Obama administration and sum it all up. You may think, well those years are gone—why revisit them? Because these are the years and the foreign policy issues that set the stage for the Washington mess amidst the Trump administration.

The first one that comes to mind is the American soldier who was detained indefinitely in Mexico. Then there were the American hostages in Iran—you know the ones we paid Iran to release. Now, we shouldn't mind if our country pays for the release of an American, but only if we have leveraged are options. Sadly, our government went through the entire process of negotiating a nuclear deal with an avowed enemy of the United States and Israel, and never exercised its right to leverage sanctions for the swap of our hostages. Another instance revolved around the soldier who was told to stand down after reporting the rape of young boys by older Afghani men at our American base in Afghanistan. Night after night our government subjected the conscience of our young men to the screams of these boys. Can you imagine? This is the trail of injustice that follows a government that takes bribes. It causes them to lose all moral footing and in turn, it leaves our brave men and women to stand against evil, alone.

At one time, America was considered a righteous nation leading the world, what happened? I am reminded of the scripture, "when the righteous are in control the people rejoice when the wicked lead the people hide." Oh, where oh where did our righteousness go? Well, not far. The very fact that Trump is challenging the corrupt status quo in Washington has embolden those who fight for righteousness—it has even caused foreign leaders to reassess their own moral integrity. Powerful.

One last memory of Obama's last four years—the humiliation our nation faced when caught spying on our allies from Merkel to Netanyahu.

Whether we realize it or not, these events shaped public opinion, and not in a positive way. We watched former President Obama draw Red Lines, Green Lines, and No lines. The blurring of these lines left our allies concerned about their national security, and Israel threatened on all sides as Iran continued to grow its terrorist networks and its nuclear arsenal.

While finishing this last chapter, I overheard the Filipino President tell former President Obama to "go to hell" on Filipino news. My heart bled. Do you comprehend the significance of that? Can you believe this is what the world thought of President Obama's worldview?

Here I sit, over a year later. President Trump just returned from a successful twelve-day Asia tour where the

United States and the Philippines publicly announced their strong alliance by releasing a joint statement of cooperation on mutual interests and shared regional challenges. Furthermore, the U.S. provided the Philippines with additional funding for counterterrorism, humanitarian needs, military security capabilities and drug demand reduction programs. That my friends are what you call steps in the right direction—wouldn't you agree?

We still have a few hurdles with our Filipino ally; sadly, Filipino President Duterte turned to the Chinese Prime Minister Xi for support after being abandoned by the Obama administration. China hailed its newly found alliance as the "golden period of fast development."

ॐ

American Restoration

Donald Trump is now the President of the United States of America. He has stepped onto a global stage desperately looking for the America that led the Free World on the heels of World War II. That America, the one that has led the Free World for the last 70 years, is a remarkable nation replete with extraordinary citizens from the four corners of the earth.

Let's peek at what a unified America accomplished in just 3.5 years to bring an end to Hitler and Japanese aggression—it's unparalleled and staggering:

During the 3.5 years of World War II, starting with the Japanese bombing of Pearl Harbor in December 1941 and ending with the surrender of Germany and Japan in 1945, the U.S. produced 22 aircraft carriers, 8 battleships, 48 cruisers, 349 destroyers, 420 destroyer escorts, 203 submarines, 34 million tons of merchants ships, 100,000 fighter aircraft, 98,00 bombers, 24,000 transport aircraft, 58,000 training aircraft, 93,000 tanks, 257,000 artillery pieces, 105,000 mortars, 3,000,000 machine guns, and 2,500,000 military trucks. America put 16.1 million men into the uniforms of various armed services. We invaded Africa, Sicily, and Italy. We won the battle for the Atlantic, planned and executed D-Day, marched across the Pacific and Europe, developed the atomic bomb and ultimately ended the wars with Japan and Germany.

Under a new season of leadership, our allies are experiencing a revived hope that America will be there for them. President Trump and his administration will continue to work towards restoring America on both Domestic and International fronts.

A declining America put the whole world in danger. At the forefront of our decline was George Soros, former President Obama, former Secretary Clinton, and many others from NGO's to foreign conspirators—as we've seen—who are not going away. But neither are we, the American people.

If we, as a nation, are willing to embrace the truth of our current state of affairs and, instead of turning a blind eye, while blaming everything on emotionally charged issues such as racism, immigration, women's rights or guns; if we face our problems with humility turning to the G-D and His human rights bill that made America and Americans great in the first place; if we forgive and forgo racial bias, hatred, or any form of divisiveness caused by global agendas, elites and self-serving interests; we can unite and come together for the common good of America. And if we would, there is no telling what we can accomplish.

And I close with these words:

"Our transport is stuck at the airport; the Libyan government is not answering. What about ours? No answer, but I am working on it."

Twelve hours after Ambassador Christ Steven's and his compound was attacked, the CIA director in Benghazi still couldn't get ahold of Washington. Where was our Secretary of State, our President, our Commander-in-Chief? We're talking about a staffed American CIA compound under siege, and no one answered the phone in Washington? That's right, no one answered. Why? They were too busy spinning spider webs, hatching cockatrice eggs and releasing vipers.

ଐ

Closing Thoughts

Daily President Trump is vilified by the media. Even while updating this book, I came across a continual stream of journalism that twisted and misrepresented Trump's vision, intent, and efforts to Make American Great Again. Why?

As you have come to learn throughout the diverse narratives of this book, all the protests over Trump's nationalism are directly and/or indirectly connected to the Soros-Obama-Clinton Network. So, of course, I won't leave you hanging—stay tuned for my next book, *The Network*, to be released in the fall of 2018.

The continual smokescreen in Washington regarding the Trump Dossier is just that, a smokescreen to keep the public's attention on Trump and off the corrupt members of both the Democratic and Republican parties. From Benghazi to Uranium One—Podesta emails to Wasserman-Schultz's IT scandal there is a trail of betrayal and corruption that is beyond the scope of this book. It's just a matter of time until truth and righteousness prevail—so don't jump ship now—the shift has only just begun. 2018 is sure to be a year of the grim reaper for all who have betrayed the American people and this great country in which we live!

What do you think should be the next move of the Trump administration? What would you like changed in

America? I would love to hear your thoughts. Let me know and I'll send you a preview of my next book!

My thought? In the spirit of restoration, justice, and equity it's time for Trump to finish unraveling the Washington Web.

&

Write me at *networkingthewhy@gmail.com*

Check out my website and courses:

www.networkingthewhy.co

Follow me on . . .

Facebook:

https://www.facebook.com/kimhadassahjohnson

Coffee with Kim:
https://www.facebook.com/groups/1796187750597095/

Twitter:

https://twitter.com/kimjohnson2on2

Instagram:

https://www.instagram.com/moveyourlifeforward/

Make sure to write a review on Amazon and register at
www.unravelingthewashingtonweb.com

To receive your free gifts as a *Thank You*

for reading my book!

ACKNOWLEDGEMENTS

෨

When I was seventeen and in my first year of college, one of the many options for a life career was writing. Becoming a journalist was high on my list of "what I wanted to be when I grew up." I'll never forget the day that my journalism professor, at Harper College, took me aside and said, "Kim you are a gifted writer. You need to give yourself to writing, develop it, and become a journalist. I believe one day you have the potential to be an excellent journalist, even a published author." I listened, filed it, and went on with life.

Truthfully, his words came with so many questions. How could I ever be a journalist or a writer? It was a mystery because I hated English and grammar and everything that was important to writing. He was right about one thing though, I loved to write. And through the years, I have written volumes of material for teaching—even published a best seller, *Teach Us to Fast and Pray*.

Each accomplishment was done by the sheer desire to help others. It never crossed my mind to "become an author or a writer." Never in my wildest dreams would a book like this be penned from my hands. And it is you, my family, friends, and fellow Americans whom I want to thank and acknowledge. Without you and your shared concerns for the future of America this book wouldn't have been written. You are my inspiration and I honor you.

I dedicated this book to my mom, Georgia Ruth Koepke. We lost you too soon, Mom, but you left us with a shared sense of love for God, love for country and love for family. All of which, coupled with your immeasurable gifts and talents, continue to bless us every day. Your life will always inspire me to greater heights.

To my Dad, Louise, Brett, Grant and Gayle and all my talented nieces and nephews—you are my family and I love you all. Dad, you are the greatest father and best friend a daughter could have, and I am so happy you remarried Louise. She is the most beautiful and loving step mother a family could ask for. And to all my crazy siblings, this book is a reality because of your unwavering support regardless of whether you liked Trump or not.

To my dearest friend Kathie Wellman, a stalwart friend who has sacrificed her own resources and time to selflessly support this endeavor. Your suggestions for deletions and editions helped immensely to ensure that I didn't chase rabbits and stayed with the issues. Not only did you edit this book, you actually read it—Thank You!

To my dear, dear, friend Anne Ney who has helped me with numerous graphic design projects throughout the years—Thank you! Your gifts and talents never cease to amaze me. And to think you helped me while writing your own book and working full time! A sacrifice I will never forget. I wish you all the success and honor.

To my dearest friends and spiritual confidants Mark and Esther Hattabaugh, and Paul and Cherith Volan (along with my two loves, Avery and Baleigh) thank you for being with me every step of the way. And to all my dear friends and family at POCC who share their concerns, love, and prayers for both America and Israel, thank you!

To my group of lifelong and new friends (and you too CWK'ers) whose faithful friendship and support never goes unnoticed! You've inspired me through every chapter. Thank you for all your calls, texts, and prayers. Especially, for staying in touch even after my poor track record for returning calls or emails while I am on the road or in the middle of writing papers for school! The list is too long to mention each of you by name—you know who you are—thank you!

I would like to make special mention of Flo Shaw, Frances and Tony Blaize, Irma and Mark Flores, Ann and Doug Klinedinst, Dea Shertzer, Carol Hudson, Vaughn and Jim Wilson, Carole Keller, MaryAnn Gulizia,

Stephanie Wagner, Mark Williams, Dyron Adams, Paul and Robin Plowman, Mae and Pincus Gilboa, Glady's Soh and Kylie Cohen. Thank you everyone for your labor of love in reading chapters, commenting, and helping me choose a book cover!

To all my friends and graduates from Glenbard East High School class of 1977. During the writing of this book we reconnected in the most amazing way. Thanks, Maryann for starting the group, and thank all of you for inspiring me through endless piles of research material!

This book would not have been possible if I had not changed the field of my Master's Degree to National Security Studies. I owe that change to three people, Dr. Alan Berger, the most eloquent and honorable professor I have been privileged to learn from. His recommendation to apply to Haifa University and continue in Holocaust Studies was the first step in altering my destiny. Secondly, the Holocaust Program at Haifa University who granted me a scholarship and the beautiful Yael Granot-Bein, program director, who helped me navigate through the difficult decision to change programs. Yael, you were the catalyst behind my transition into the National Security Studies program and I will be forever grateful. And thirdly, Dan Shueftan, the director of the National Security Studies Program; you deserve a special mention. Twenty years ago, you were a guest speaker for a three-day conference on Israeli National Security. It was hosted by the Chicago Jewish Federation. You taught a masterpiece on terrorism that I never forgot. I remember leaning over to my friend and saying, we're going to Haifa to study with Dan Shueftan. Who knew that those words would land me in this amazing program twenty years later. It's a story that one day will be shared. After joining this program, something clicked—like the last piece of a puzzle is placed into the picture. Thank you, Dan—for the call and accepting me into the program—it has changed my life.

To Rachel Suissa, my professor who took the time to read many chapters in this book and write a review. Your guidance through the deep waters of Middle Eastern theory has opened to me a whole new world of understanding.

To my mentor, Brendon Burchard. I thank G-D for connecting me with you and your life's work to help others succeed. Your influence is the single most important reason this book exists. Your high performance and marketing training has changed the way I structure my ideas, goals, time, and talents. What a game changer you are and continue to be in my life. Thanks, Brendon!

Lastly, to Bill Mehlman my dearest friend whose life as a prolific author, editor, journalist and columnist has set the bar of excellence in my life. I have yet to meet anyone who writes with such clarity of purpose and mastery of words like you Bill. Thank you, Bill for your ideas and encouragement throughout the writing of this book. May your love for America, Israel and the Almighty be rewarded!

"The greatest gift of life is friendship, and I have received it."

Hubert H. Humphrey

ൟ

ABOUT THE AUTHOR

℘

I don't know anyone who likes to write about themselves. Where do you begin and where do you end? About the author is more than a CV, it's a portrait. When you look at an individual portrait, one painted by a good artist, you sense that you are meeting someone. And when you walk away you feel as if you have just peeked behind the curtain of their life, even if it's just on the surface.

Some say it's being you on paper and others say it's being the you you've always wanted to be. I say it's about sharing yourself with the reader. Sharing the person behind the pen in a way that the reader can connect and relate. So here I go.

Have you ever thought that you were on this earth for a reason? When I was in my early twenties I asked G-D three things: Who are you? What is your name? and What is my purpose? And He answered me—not immediately but over time. In doing so, He so graciously gifted me with His presence and His Spirit. I became a sponge for knowledge and understanding the *why* of life.

Oftentimes, the when, the where, and even the how can easily be extracted from a subject or current event, but the "why" is often a mystery: An obscure thread of inter-connected events and ideological developments that lend themselves to an outcome. Understanding the "why" helps us to navigate through life's surprises. It enables us to make intelligent choices. And it heals us. It heals our hearts, relationships, and history. It heals the individual as well as the collective conscience. Yes, answering the "why" is the secret to understanding! Solomon wrote in Proverbs 4:7, "Wisdom is the principal thing; therefore, get wisdom: and with all thy getting get understanding."

In a sublime way, this book, my blog, online classes, and even products are about "networking the why."

As for my education—I dropped out of college in my second year because of a broken relationship and a new career in the printing industry. Making money was much more fun than going to school. I went on to great success in the industry and at the age of 23, I became the first woman to invited to speak at the annual gravure and lithographic conferences. By 24, I sat on the board of directors of one small company and was running a second marketing company on the side. All of that came to an end due to ethical choices I made along with a newly found direction after having a life changing encounter with G-D.

From the age of 25 until today, my life has been about learning, teaching, and advocating for Jewish-Christian relations and studies, as well as U.S.-Israel relations and studies. The emergence of national Israel, in 1948, was a game changer for the entire world! And with it, a theological upheaval within all monotheistic faiths: Judaism, Christianity and Islam! Understanding *why Israel,* along with all its caveats, is the essence of my work for the last thirty years.

At 50 I returned to college. I completed my AA in Jewish studies as well as obtained several certificates in the field of Multi-Media Authoring from Broward College. I went on to finish my undergraduate degree at Florida Atlantic University where I graduated Magna Cum Laude with a B.A. in Jewish Studies and History. In 2017, I completed my M.A. degree in National Security Studies from Haifa University, Israel. What's next? Make sure you get on my email list to find out!

Two years ago, www.NetworkingtheWhy.co, my blog www.kimhjohnson.com and Coffee with Kim Live were created to answer the why and share insights on *this, that and the other.* Often, I wake up with an experience, thought, or idea that could help or inspire others and I want to share it!

When the Trump-Clinton election cycle began, I wanted to help, but didn't know what to do. Almost daily I was getting these "brain downloads" of Donald Trump's policy views. It was the craziest thing. I would write them down in speech form before he would ever speak on them, of course in a politer manner. Nevertheless, after writing a few of them, I knew he was going to be the next President of the United States. G-D wouldn't waste my time by foretelling me stuff that wasn't going to happen. Ultimately, that experience led me to writing this book

I know this book is controversial and may offend some people, and for that I'm sorry. But truth is a two-edged sword; it both hurts and heals. I have addressed issues central to the future of America. I have endeavored to show that our nation's core values are under assault; even being hijacked by individuals and organizations that want America marginalized, if not destroyed. Evil is never what it appears to be. It's often cloaked in promise and progress. And for it to dissipate it must be exposed.

America's not perfect, but she is destined to be great again. Not because of American exceptionalism or a tolerant democracy, a leading capitalistic society or individual distinction, but because she is a covenant nation brimming with life. She takes in the tired and the weary, the poor and the needy; all of whom desire to make a difference. Her laws are righteous, and her ways are unique to any nation in the world. And above all, she offers every immigrant and every citizen a future and hope for tomorrow. And as an American, you are either for her or against her. And it is time for those who are against her to step aside, get out of her way, because she's ready for a resurrection!

Wishing you Kol Hakavod and b'hatzlacha (בהצלחה)! All the Honor and Success! Make sure to leave your comments on Amazon.

Thank you for taking the time to read *Unraveling the Washington Web*. I look forward to hearing from you!

ഇൽ

We are not now that strength which in old days moved earth and heaven. That which we are we are. One equal temper of heroic hearts made weak by time and fate, but strong in will to strive, to seek, to find and not to yield.

Alfred Tennyson

ဆာ

NOTES

മ

[1] Daniel 2:22, Deuteronomy 29:29, Isaiah 45:19

[2] Isaiah 59:8

[3] Isaiah 59:14-15

[4] Fastest striking snake
http://www.animaldanger.com/australia.php

[5] ibid.

[6] Steiner, Amanda M. (2015, June 29). *Your Fired: NBC Drops Miss Universe and Miss USA After Donald Trump's Comments About Mexican Immigrants.* Retrieved from http://www.people.com/article/nbc-drops-donald-trump-miss-universe-miss-usa

[7] Boston, Claire. (2015, July 2). *Serta Will Stop Selling Trump Mattress Line In Latest Defection.* Retrieved from http://www.bloomberg.com/politics/articles/2015-07-01/serta-will-stop-selling-trump-mattress-line-in-latest-defection

[8]Walker, Hunter. (2015, July 6). *Donald Trump just released an epic statement raging against Mexican immigrants and 'disease.'* Retrieved from http://www.businessinsider.com/donald-trumps-epic-statement-on-mexico-2015-7

[9] Carusone, Angelo. *Tell Macy's: Dump Donald Trump.* Retrieved from http://petitions.moveon.org/sign/urge-macys-to-dump-donald

[10] Nimmo, Kurt. (2016, March 12). *Soros funded moveone.org takes credit for violence in Chicago.* Retrieved from http://www.infowars.com/soros-funded-moveon-org-takes-credit-for-violence-in-chicago/

[11] Kiely, Eugene. (2012, April 19). *The Facts About 'Fat Cats.'* Retrieved from http://www.factcheck.org/2012/04/the-facts-about-fat-cats/

[12] http://www.politifact.com/personalities/moveon/

Even the post-election change.org petition, "Electoral [13] College: Make Hillary Clinton on December 19" has his signature all over it. Frye, Patrick. (2016, March 13). *George Soros— Funded moveon.org Takes Responsibility For Violent Donald Trump Protest—Promises More Protests To Come.* Retrieved from http://www.inquisitr.com/2885453/george-soros-funded-moveon-org-takes-responsibility-for-violent-donald-trump-protest-promises-more-protests-are-to-come/

[14] McClure-Davidson, Vicki. (2010, September 7). *Profile of a Liberal Sociopath: Billionaire George Soros Helped Nazis Murder & Steal From Jews, Feels No Remorse or Guilt.* Retrieved from http://www.frugal-cafe.com/public_html/frugal-blog/frugal-cafe-

blogzone/2010/09/07/profile-of-a-liberal-sociopath-billionaire-george-soros-helped-nazis-murder-steal-from-jews-feels-no-remorse-or-guilt/

[15] McClure Davidson, Vicki. (2011, January 28th). *George Soros Says He Feels No Remorse For Collaborating With Nazis During WWII to Send His Fellow Jews to the Death Camps, Steal Their Property.* Retrieved from http://itmakessenseblog.com/2011/01/28/george-soros-says-he-feels-no-remorse-for-collaborating-with-nazis-during-wwii-to-send-his-fellow-jews-to-the-death-camps-steal-their-property/

[16] Geller, Pamella. (2006, October 30). *The Judenrat Soros.* Retrieved from http://pamelageller.com/2006/10/the_judenrat_so-1.html/ In an interview with 60 minutes Soros, responding to a statement of him watching lots of Jews get shipped off to death camps, said,"Right. I was 14 years old. And I would say that that's when my character was made."

[17] http://message.snopes.com/showthread.php?t=43876

[18] Geller, Pamella. (2006, October 11). *Soros and the Nazis Undermining the Jewish People.* Retrieve from http://pamelageller.com/2006/10/soros_and_the_n.html/

[19] Geller, Pamella. (2006, October 11). *Soros and the Nazis Undermining the Jewish People.* Retrieved from http://pamelageller.com/2006/10/soros_and_the_n.html/#sthash.3WQ64AGG.dpuf

[20] Geller, Pamella. (2006, October 11). *Soros and the Nazis Undermining the Jewish People.* Retrieved from http://pamelageller.com/2006/10/soros_and_the_n.html/#sthash.3WQ64AGG.dpuf

[21] Druden, Tyler. (2015, July 2). Hacked Emails Expose George Soros As Ukraine Puppet Master. Retrieved from http://www.zerohedge.com/news/2015-06-01/hacked-emails-expose-george-soros-ukraine-puppet-master

[22] Browne, Clayton. (2015, May 20). *Soros Says China Is A Major Risk For World War 3*. Retrieved from http://www.valuewalk.com/2015/05/soros-china-is-risk-for-world-war-3/

[23] Druden, Tyler. (2015, May 22). *George Soros Warns, "No Exaggeration" That China-US On "Threshold of World War3."* Retrieved from http://www.zerohedge.com/news/2015-05-21/george-soros-warns-no-exaggeration-china-us-threshold-world-war-3

[24] Parry, Robert. (2016, April 5). *'Corruption' as a Propoganda Weapon.* Retreived from http://www.globalresearch.ca/corruption-as-a-propaganda-weapon/5518663

[25] Corcoran, Kieran. (2015, January 16). *Billionaire George Soros spent 33 million bankrolling Ferguson demonstrators create 'echo chamber' drive national protests.* Retrieved from http://www.dailymail.co.uk/news/article-2913625/Billionaire-George-Soros-spent-33MILLION-bankrolling-Ferguson-demonstrators-create-echo-chamber-drive-national-protests.html#ixzz4EqPYLzLT

[26] Riddell, Kelly. (2015, January 14). *George Soros funds Ferguson protests, hopes to spur civil action.* Retrieved from http://www.washingtontimes.com/news/2015/jan/14/george-soros-funds-ferguson-protests-hopes-to-spur/

[27] Riddell, Kelly. (2015, January 14). *George Soros funds Ferguson protests, hopes to spur civil action.* Retrieved from http://www.washingtontimes.com/news/2015/jan/14/george-soros-funds-ferguson-protests-hopes-to-spur/

[28] Teshuva means, "to return." Specifically, taking words or an answer to your actions and retuning to God.

[29] Editor. (2016, April 5). *Geopolitiks of Corruption: George Soros and the 'Panama Leaks.'* Retrieved from http://www.theeventchronicle.com/panama-papers/geopolitics-corruption-george-soros-panama-leaks/#

[30] Highlighted in the Panama Paper leaks were Russia's Vladimir Putin indirectly, and more specifically his best friend, Sergei Roldugin. Also taken to task were the father of British Prime Minister David Cameron, Argentinian President Mauricio Macri (who is pro-American) and former Presidents Cristina and Nestor Kirchner. The list continues with Ukranian and Azerbejain Presidents Poroshenko and Aliyev, Saudi King Salaman, former Emir of Qatar, and current President of the United Arab Emirates. It also included the former Prime Minister of China and several other large Chinese officials.

[31] Editor. (2016, April 5). *Geopolitiks of Corruption: George Soros and the 'Panama Leaks.'* Retrieved from http://www.theeventchronicle.com/panama-papers/geopolitics-corruption-george-soros-panama-leaks/#

[32] https://answers.yahoo.com/question/index?qid=20100826172157AA3mewa

[33] Other reports mark the recent visit of George Soros with Robert Malley as his 13th time. Watson, Steve. (2016, March 2). *Soros Met With Obama's top ISIS Advisor Last Month.*

Retrieved from http://www.infowars.com/soros-met-with-obamas-top-isis-advisor-last-month-2/

[34]Rob Malley's tenure will end in January 2017 when President elect Trump replaces the Obama administration.

[35] Safian, Alex. (2015, March 11). *Robert Malley and US Policy on Israel*. Retrieved from http://www.camera.org/index.asp?x_context=8&x_nameinnews=88&x_article=2962

[36] https://en.wikipedia.org/wiki/Robert_Malley

[37] Watson, Steve. (2016, March 2). *Soros Met With Obama's top ISIS Advisor Last Month.* Retrieved from http://www.infowars.com/soros-met-with-obamas-top-isis-advisor-last-month-2/

[38] Sainato, Michael. (2016, August 15). *DC Leak Exposes Top Clinton Donor George Soros Manipulating Elections.* Retrieved from http://observer.com/2016/08/dc-leak-exposes-top-clinton-donor-george-soros-manipulating-elections/

[39] Ehrenfeld, Rachel, Macomber, Shawn. (2004, October 4). Rachel Ehrenfeld is the author of "Funding Evil" (Bonus Books, 2003). Shawn Macomber is a staff writer at the American Spectator. *George Soros: The 'God' Who Carries Around Some Dangerous Demons.* Retrieved from http://articles.latimes.com/2004/oct/04/opinion/oe-ehrenfeld4

[40] *"Kate's Law" and the License To Hate.* (2016, April 27). Retrieved from http://www.huffingtonpost.com/samanta-honigman/kates-law-and-the-license_b_9789508.html

[41] Homeland Security. (2009, July 21) *ICE. Secure Communities: A Comprehensive Plan to Identify and Remove*

Criminal Aliens (Strategic Plan). Retrieved from
https://www.ice.gov/doclib/foia/secure_communities/secureco
mmunitiesstrategicplan09.pdf

[42] Preston. Julia. (2009, November 12) *U.S. Identifies 111,000 Immigrants With Criminal Records.* Retrieved from
http://www.nytimes.com/2009/11/13/us/13ice.html

[43] Homeland Security. (2009, July 21) *ICE. Secure Communities: A Comprehensive Plan to Identify and Remove Criminal Aliens (Strategic Plan).* Retrieved from
https://www.ice.gov/doclib/foia/secure_communities/secureco
mmunitiesstrategicplan09.pdf

[44] Preston, Julia. (2011, August 13). *Resistance Widens to Obama Initiative on Criminal Immigrants.*
http://www.nytimes.com/2011/08/13/us/politics/13secure.html
?_r=1&ref=us

[45] Thau, David. (2012, January) *Immigration and the Failure of Federalism.* Journal of Civil Rights and Economic Development: Issue 2 Volume 26, Winter 2012, Issue 2. p. 518. "[T]he National Immigration and Customs Enforcement Council-an AFL-CIO affiliate-and affiliated local councils cast a unanimous 259-0 vote of no confidence in ICE Director John Morton and Assistant Director Phyllis Coven." Retrieval from
http://scholarship.law.stjohns.edu/cgi/viewcontent.cgi?article=
1708&context=jcred

[46] Seper, Jerry. (2010, August 9). *Agents' union disavows leaders of ICE.* Retrieved from
http://www.washingtontimes.com/news/2010/aug/9/agents-
union-disavows-leaders-of-ice/

[47] Homeland Security. (2009, July 21) *ICE. Secure Communities: A Comprehensive Plan to Identify and Remove Criminal Aliens (Strategic Plan)*. Retrieved from https://www.ice.gov/doclib/foia/secure_communities/secureco mmunitiesstrategicplan09.pdf

[48] Preston, Julia. (2012, January 7). *Agents' Union Stalls Training on Deportation Rules. Retrieved from* http://www.nytimes.com/2012/01/08/us/illegal-immigrants-who-commit-crimes-focus-of-deportation.html?pagewanted=all

[49] Steinlight, Stephen. (2012, January 11). *National ICE Council Freezes the Obama Blitz.* Center for Immigration Studies. http://cis.org/steinlight/national-ICE-council-freezes-the-obama-blitz

[50] Pear, Robert. (2011, August 18). *Fewer Youths to Be Deported in New Policy*. Retrieved from http://www.nytimes.com/2011/08/19/us/19immig.html

[51] BBC News. (2011, August 18) *US Will Review 300,000 Immigration Deportation Cases*. Retrieved from http://www.bbc.co.uk/news/world-us-canada-14585238

[52] Synder, Michael. (2013, August 19). *Obama Administration Makes Secret Deal With Mexico To Help Illegal Immigrants In The Workplace*. Retrieved from http://endoftheamericandream.com/archives/obama-administration-makes-secret-deal-with-mexico-to-help-illegal-immigrants-in-the-workplace

[53] Grandoni, Dino. (2011, September 9). *Obama Administration Nears Its Millionth Deportation*, The Atlantic Wire. Retrieved from

http://www.thewire.com/national/2011/09/obama-administration-nears-its-millionth-deportation/42302/

[54] Manuel, Jens, Passel J., Cohn, D. (2016, November 3). *5 facts about illegal immigration in the U.S.* Retrieved from http://www.pewresearch.org/fact-tank/2015/11/19/5-facts-about-illegal-immigration-in-the-u-s/

[55] Chambers, Francesca. (2016, June 30). *Obama launches an extraordinary rant against Trump's 'xenophobia' and 'disregard for workers' - as he insists 'I care about poor people'.* Retrieved from http://www.dailymail.co.uk/news/article-3666104/Obama-s-anti-Trump-huddles-Mexican-leader-compared-Republican-Hitler-Canada-s-liberal-pin-mocked-Clinton-rival.html#ixzz4DTH77zUr

[56] Adam Liptak. (2012, June 25). *Blocking Parts of Arizona Law, Justices Allow Its Centerpiece.* Retrieved From http://www.nytimes.com/2012/06/26/us/supreme-court-rejects-part-of-arizona-immigration-law.html

[57] Adam Liptak. (2012, June 25). *Blocking Parts of Arizona Law, Justices Allow Its Centerpiece.* Retrieved From http://www.nytimes.com/2012/06/26/us/supreme-court-rejects-part-of-arizona-immigration-law.html

[58] Adam Liptak. (2012, June 25). *Blocking Parts of Arizona Law, Justices Allow Its Centerpiece.* Retrieved From http://www.nytimes.com/2012/06/26/us/supreme-court-rejects-part-of-arizona-immigration-law.html

[59] Adam Liptak. (2012, June 25). *Blocking Parts of Arizona Law, Justices Allow Its Centerpiece.* Retrieved From

http://www.nytimes.com/2012/06/26/us/supreme-court-rejects-part-of-arizona-immigration-law.html

[60] Radia, Kirit. (2013, April 20). *Boston Bomb Suspect Alarmed Russian Relatives With Extremist Views.* Retrieved from http://abcnews.go.com/US/boston-bomb-suspect-alarmed-russian-relatives-extremist-views/story?id=19006449

[61] Buncombe, Andrew. (2016, June 19). *Donald Trump Says US Should Consider Profiling Muslims.* Retrieved from http://www.independent.co.uk/news/world/americas/us-elections/donald-trump-says-us-should-consider-profiling-muslims-a7090731.html

[62] http://www.foxnews.com/us/2017/11/01/nyc-terror-attack-leaves-8-dead-several-injured-suspects-notes-pledged-isis-loyalty.html

[63] https://heavy.com/news/2017/10/sayfullo-saipov-manhattan-truck-ramming-suspect-terror/

[64] http://www.nj.com/passaic-county/index.ssf/2017/11/south_paterson_unleashes_on_animal_ny_terror_suspect_as_fbi_swarms_community.html

[65] https://www.donaldjtrump.com/positions/pay-for-the-wall

[66] https://www.fincen.gov/statutes_regs/patriot/

[67] http://www.foxnews.com/politics/2017/09/21/trumps-border-wall-look-at-numbers.html

[68] Colangelo, Lisa, Pearson, E. (2016, April 23). *Immigrants from Dominican Republic, Ecuador share their Citizenship NOW! success stories.* Retrieved from

http://www.nydailynews.com/new-york/immigrants-share-citizenship-success-stories-article-1.2612116

[69] Written by Kim Johnson

[70] Brown, Tim. (2015, May 11). *1,063 Documented Examples of Barack Obama's Lying, Lawbreaking, Corruption, Cronyism, Hypocrisy, Waste, Etc.* Retrieved from http://freedomoutpost.com/1063-documented-examples-of-barack-obamas-lying-lawbreaking-corruption-cronyism-hypocrisy-waste-etc/

[71] Alman, Daniel. (2009-2016, May). *1,304 well sourced examples of Barack Obama's lying, lawbreaking, corruption, cronyism, hypocrisy, waste, etc.* Retrieved from https://danfromsquirrelhill.wordpress.com/2013/08/15/obama-252/

[72] http://www.wikihow.com/Spot-a-Pathological-Liar

[73] Hill, Tamara. *6 Subtle Characteristics of The Pathological Liar.* Retrieved from http://blogs.psychcentral.com/caregivers/2014/09/6-subtle-characteristics-of-the-pathological-liar/

[74] Johnson, Charles, C. (2016, July 6). *CONFIRMED: Bloods Gangbanger, Democrat #AltonSterling Owned Illegal Gun, Had Drug, Assault Weapon Convictions.* Retrieved from http://gotnews.com/confirmed-bloods-gangbanger-altonsterling-owned-illegal-gun-drug-gun-convictions/

[75] McBride, Jessica. (2016, July 6). *Alton Sterling Arrest Record, Criminal History & Rap Sheet [DOCUMENTS].* Retrieved from http://heavy.com/news/2016/07/alton-sterling-arrest-record-criminal-history-rap-sheet-sex-offender-sex-

offense-crime-baton-rouge-louisiana-police-shooting-blane-salamoni-howie-lake-shot-charges-video-youtube-facebook-watch/

[76] Hill, Tamara. *6 Subtle Characteristics of The Pathological Liar*. Retrieved from http://blogs.psychcentral.com/caregivers/2014/09/6-subtle-characteristics-of-the-pathological-liar/

[77] Alman, Daniel. (2009-2016, May). *1,304 well sourced examples of Barack Obama's lying, lawbreaking, corruption, cronyism, hypocrisy, waste, etc.* Retrieved from https://danfromsquirrelhill.wordpress.com/2013/08/15/obama-252/

[78]https://web.archive.org/web/20101119082141/http://www.washingtonexaminer.com/politics/Former-lobbyists-in-senior-Obama-administration-positions-83362902.html#ixzz4FXWe0xzY This article may require a password or sign up with the Washington Examiner. Articles that confirm this information include endnote 73. Here are two other "must reads" if you are interested in this lobby issues by Timothy Carney: Retrieved from http://www.washingtonexaminer.com/article/2562038 and http://www.washingtonexaminer.com/obama-hires-revolving-door-lobbyist-and-clinton-fixer-john-podesta/article/2540496

[79] Carney, Timothy. (2013, July 23). *Obama administration packed with lobbyists he vowed not to hire.* Retrieved from http://www.washingtonexaminer.com/obama-administration-packed-with-lobbyists-he-vowed-not-to-hire/article/2533397 Carney and McGrath cite over 100 lobbyists hired during the Obama Administration.

[80] https://www.activistfacts.com/organizations/528-center-for-american-progress/

[81] Sargent, Greg. (2009, March 10). *Center For American Progress Launching Big War Room To Drive Obama Agenda.* Retrieved from http://www.sourcewatch.org/index.php/Center_for_American_Progress

[82] Alman, Daniel. (2009-2016, May). *1,304 well sourced examples of Barack Obama's lying, lawbreaking, corruption, cronyism, hypocrisy, waste, etc.* https://danfromsquirrelhill.wordpress.com/2013/08/15/obama-252/

[83] Alman, Daniel. (2009-2016, May). *1,304 well sourced examples of Barack Obama's lying, lawbreaking, corruption, cronyism, hypocrisy, waste, etc.* Items 501 through 1,000 can be found at https://danfromsquirrelhill.wordpress.com/2015/12/04/obama-part-2/

[84] Alman, Daniel. (2009-2016, May). *1,304 well sourced examples of Barack Obama's lying, lawbreaking, corruption, cronyism, hypocrisy, waste, etc.* Items 1,001 through 1,249 can be found at https://danfromsquirrelhill.wordpress.com/2015/12/04/obama-part-3/

[85] Deuteronomy 1:15-16, "So I took the chief of your tribes, wise men, and known, and made them heads over you, captains over thousands, and captains over hundreds, and captains over fifties, and captains over tens, and officers among your tribes. And I charged your judges at that time, saying Hear the causes

between your brethren, and judge righteously between every man ands brother, and the stranger that is with him."

86 Deuteronomy 11:24-25

87 The book of Jeremiah chapter 31

88 https://www.archives.gov/founding-docs

89 Hormandi, Dan. (2014, April 30). *George Washington's Covenant with God.* Retrieved from https://lessonsfromthefounders.wordpress.com/2014/04/30/289/

90 https://www.billofrightsinstitute.org/founding-documents/bill-of-rights/

91 Spalding, Matthew. Eberly, D., Gregg, S., Loconte, J. Building *a Culture of Character.* Retrieved from http://www.heritage.org/research/lecture/building-a-culture-of-character

92 Spalding, Matthew. Eberly, D., Gregg, S., Loconte, J. *Building a Culture of Character.* Retrieved from http://www.heritage.org/research/lecture/building-a-culture-of-character

93 http://www.diffen.com/difference/Anti-Federalist_vs_Federalist

94 https://www.billofrightsinstitute.org/founding-documents/bill-of-rights/

95 Kopstein Jeffrey, Lichbach, M. (2000). *Comparative Politics: Interests, Identities, and Institutions in a Changing Global Order.* Cambridge UP. p. 72. Retrieved from

https://www.scribd.com/doc/55305065/Comparative-Politics-Interests-Identities-and-Institutions

[96] McLean, Iain. *Thomas Jefferson, John Adams, and the Déclaration des Droits de l'Homme et du Citoyen* in *The future of liberal democracy: Thomas Jefferson and the contemporary world* (Palgrave Macmillan, 2004) online Retrieved from http://www.palgraveconnect.com/pc/doifinder/10.1057/978140 3981455

[97] Benjamin Franklin (2003). *The Political Thought of Benjamin Franklin*. Edited by Ralph Ketcham; Hackett Publishing. p. 398. Available at https://www.hackettpublishing.com/the-political-thought-of-benjamin-franklin

[98] *The Declaration of the Rights of Man and of the Citizen*. Retrieved from http://avalon.law.yale.edu/18th_century/rightsof.asp

[99] There are those who believe Hegel's idea originated with Immanuel Kant

[100] Georg F. W. Hegel (1770-1831) was a major figure in German idealism.

[101] Popper, Karl R. (1971). *The Open Society, and Its Enemies: The High Tide of Prophecy: Hegel, Marx, and the Aftermath*, 2 vols. 5th rev. ed. Princeton, NJ: Princeton University Press, [1966] 1971, 2:31.

[102] Some scholars dispute the authenticity of Rauschning's recounting of his time with Hitler. Richard Steigmann-Gall considered Rauschning's *Hitler Speaks* (1939), published in America as *The Voice of Destruction*, "to be fraudulent." (*The

Holy Reich: Nazi Conceptions of Christianity, 1919-1945 [New York: Cambridge University Press, 2003], 29). There doesn't seem to be anything out of character in what Rauschning wrote. Hitler did do away with the Ten Commandments. Hitler was at war with the Old Testament. Others saw the true Hitler before Rauschning. See Cardinal Faulhaber, *Judaism, Christianity and Germany* (London: Burns Oates & Washbourne Ltd., 1934). Then there are the public statements of Martin Bormann (1900-1945?), head of the Party Chancellery and Hitler's private secretary: "National Socialist and Christian concepts are incompatible. . . . Our National Socialist world view stands on a much higher level than the concepts of Christianity, which in their essentials were taken over from Judaism. For this reason, too, we can do without Christianity." (Martin Bormann, "National Socialist and Christian Concepts Are Incompatible" [1937], *Nazi Culture: Intellectual, Cultural andSocial Life in the Third Reich*, George L. Mosse [New York: Grosset & Dunlap, 1968], 244). Retrieved from http://www.rightlydividingtheword.com/articles/battle_against _the_ten_commandments.htm

[103] http://www.age-of-the-sage.org/philosophy/friedrich_nietzsche_quotes.html

[104] Rauschning, "Preface," xiii. *The Ten Commandments: Ten Short Novels of Hitler's War Against The Moral Code. New York*: Simon and Schuester, 1943. Hitler's statement was recounted by Rauschning while spending the evening with him and other Nazi party loyalists at the Reich Chancery. Retrieved from http://www.rightlydividingtheword.com/articles/battle_against _the_ten_commandments.htm

[105] Herbert Huffmon, (2004) *The Fundamental Code Illustrated: The Third Commandment, in* The Ten Commandments: The Reciprocity of Faithfulness, ed. William P. Brown., pp. 205–212. Westminster John Knox Press. *The author added a*dditional text for continuity of thought.

[106] Romans 13:8-10

[107] Rauschning, Hermann (1887- 1982), was a German Conservative Revolutionary who broke with the Nazi party and fled from Germany in 1936. He served as a German officer in WWI and spent the years of WWII denouncing Hitler and the Nazi agenda.

[108] Mann, Thomas, et.al. *The Ten Commandments: Ten Short Novels of Hitler's War Against The Moral Code. New York*: Simon and Schuester, 1943

[109] http://time.com/3508291/china-underground-churches-catholicism-catholics-christianity-christians-kevin-frayer/

[110] http://www.jewishtimesasia.org/shanghai/262-shanghai-communities/46-shanghai-china-jewish-community

[111] Torah is the first five books of the Bible. It lays the foundation of God's government in the earth and His moral laws to govern humanity in a just and righteous manner.

[112] *1968: The Year That Changed History.* Retrieved from https://www.theguardian.com/observer/gallery/2008/jan/17/1

[113] http://www.historynet.com/vietnam-war

[114] Tet Offensive

[115] 1968: Timeline. Retrieved from http://cds.library.brown.edu/projects/1968/reference/timeline.html

[116] 1968: Timeline. Retrieved from http://cds.library.brown.edu/projects/1968/reference/timeline.html

[117] Torry, Jack. (2008, March 30). *Chaotic 1968 Changed America Forever*. Retrieved from http://www.dispatch.com/content/stories/insight/2008/03/30/1968.ART_ART_03-30-08_G1_JL9OP2U.html

[118] Kurlansky, Mark. (2004). *1968: the Year that Rocked the World.* Available at https://www.amazon.com/1968-Year-That-Rocked-World/dp/0345455827

[119] Rauschning, "Preface," xiii. *The Ten Commandments: Ten Short Novels of Hitler's War Against The Moral Code.* New York: Simon and Schuester, 1943. Hitler's statement was recounted by Rauschning while spending the evening with him and other Nazi party loyalists at the Reich Chancery.

[120] Browne, Clayton. (2015, May 20). *Soros Says China Is Major Risk For World War 3.* Retrieved from http://www.valuewalk.com/2015/05/soros-china-is-risk-for-world-war-3/

[121] ibid.

[122] Isaiah 10:14

[123] Miller, D. (1997). *Sir Karl Raimund Popper, C. H., F. B. A. 28 July 1902--17 September 1994. Elected F.R.S. 1976.* Biographical Memoirs of Fellows of the Royal Society. **43**: 369–310. doi:10.1098/rsbm.1997.0021

[124] Popper archives fasc. 297.11

[125] See also Karl Popper: On freedom. *All life is problem solving* (1999), chapter 7, p. 81f

[126] Soros, George. (1995). *Soros on Soros: Staying Ahead of the Curve.* New York, Wiley. pp. 253-263 Retrieved from http://eu.wiley.com/WileyCDA/WileyTitle/productCd-0471119776.html

[127] Acts 17: 23-28

[128] Popper, Karl. (1947). *The Open Society and Its Enemies: The Spell of Plato. Volume 1*, George Routledge & Sons, ltd., pp. 226, (1971) p. 265. *Complete Volumes I & II* (1966), p. 581

[129] http://shariahthethreat.org/a-short-course-1-what-is-shariah/

[130] http://islam.stackexchange.com/questions/4254/what-is-the-difference-between-hadith-and-Qur'an

[131] Qutb, Sayyid. (2005). *Milestones*, p. Dar al-llm., Damascus, Syria. p. 110-111

[132] There are one or two examples of reformation within Sharia law that appears to allow for a more liberal approach towards human rights thus appeasing the United Nations Human Rights Council. But don't be fooled. Islamists are allowed to use lying and deceptive techniques to achieve their goals. Hence, even if there is a human rights compromise, the concept of jihad and overthrowing democracy is still the ultimate aim of all that promote Sharia law as compatible within the framework of a national government.

[133] *Shariah: The Threat to America.* Retrieved from https://www.centerforsecuritypolicy.org/upload/wysiwyg/article%20pdfs/Shariah%20-

%20The%20Threat%20to%20America%20(Team%20B%20R eport)%20Web%2009292010.pdf

[134] Psalm 9:17

[135] Capehart, Jonathan. (2012, June 20). *Pelosi defends her infamous health care remark.*
https://www.washingtonpost.com/blogs/post-partisan/post/pelosi-defends-her-infamous-health-care-remark/2012/06/20/gJQAqch6qV_blog.html?utm_term=.68e93 afb1d37

[136] ibid.

[137] 2009 figures1,990. Retrieved from
http://computationallegalstudies.com/2009/11/08/facts-about-the-length-of-h-r-3962/

[138] Kessler, Glenn. (2013, May 15). *How many pages of regulations for 'Obamacare'?* 2013 numbers range from 20,000 to 33,000. Retrieved from
https://www.washingtonpost.com/blogs/fact-checker/post/how-many-pages-of-regulations-for-obamacare/2013/05/14/61eec914-bcf9-11e2-9b09-1638acc3942e_blog.html

[139] Yoo, John. (2016, February 8). *A Call For Action Against Government Overreach.* Retrieved from
https://www.aei.org/publication/a-call-for-action-against-government-overreach/

[140] Shapiro, Ilya. (2013, December 23). *President Obama's Top 10 Constitutional Violations of 2013.* Retrieved from
http://www.forbes.com/sites/realspin/2013/12/23/president-

obamas-top-10-constitutional-violations-of-
2013/#183f5f7e41bf

[141] Shapiro, Ilya. (2015, December 23). *President Obama's Top Ten Constitutional Violations of 2015.* Retrieved from http://www.nationalreview.com/article/428882/obama-violate-constitution-top-ten-2015

[142] https://www.oyez.org/cases/2011/11-393 The ACA contained a minimum coverage provision by amending the tax code and providing an individual mandate, stipulating that by 2014, non-exempt individuals who failed to purchase and maintain a minimum level of health insurance must pay a tax penalty. The ACA also contained an expansion of Medicaid, which States had to accept to receive Federal funds for Medicaid, and an employer mandate to obtain health coverage for employees.

[143] https://ballotpedia.org/Obamacare_lawsuits

[144] https://ballotpedia.org/Obamacare_lawsuits#cite_note-40

[145] *42 U.S. Code § 2000bb–1 - Free exercise of religion protected.* Retrieved from https://www.law.cornell.edu/uscode/text/42/2000bb-1

[146] Bratek, Rebecca. (2104, July 19). *Law firm in Hobby Lobby win is playing key role in religion cases.* Retrieved from http://www.latimes.com/nation/la-na-becket-fund-20140720-story.html

[147] Childers, Karl. (2014, March 27). *Hobby Lobby Case Opens TheDoor To Islam Sharia Law Be Careful What Ya Wish.* Retrieved from http://liberalforum.net/viewtopic.php?t=4224&p=211574

[148] Clifton, Allen. (2014, July 2). *George Takei: What if Muslims Owned Hobby Lobby and Tried Imposing Sharia Law on Employees?* Retrieved from http://www.forwardprogressives.com/george-takei-muslims-owned-hobby-lobby-tried-forcing-sharia-law-employees/

[149] Drobnic Holan, Angie. (2013, May 30). *'Dhimmitude' on page 107 of the health care law exempts Muslims, claims chain email.* Retrieved from http://www.politifact.com/truth-o-meter/statements/2013/may/30/chain-email-dhimmitude-page-107-health-care-law-exempts-muslim/

[150] Burns, Eric. (2011, October 13). *Muslims Exempt From Obamacare?* Retrieved from http://www.frontpagemag.com/fpm/108489/muslims-exempt-obamacare-eric-burns

[151] ibid.

[152] http://obamacarefacts.com/healthcare-sharing-ministry-exemptions/

[153] Burns, Eric. (2011, October 13). *Muslims Exempt From Obamacare?* Retrieved from http://www.frontpagemag.com/fpm/108489/muslims-exempt-obamacare-eric-burns

[154] *AIG Offers First Takaful Homeowners Insurance Product for U.S.* (2008, December 2). Retrieved from http://www.insurancejournal.com/news/national/2008/12/02/95930.htm

[155] Macfarlane, Benjamin. *Shariah Compliant Insurance Products – Takaful in the UK.* Retrieved from http://www.bjm-co.com/reports/Article_006_Takaful_150605_101k.pdf

[156] *Islamic Finance: Ethics, Concepts, Practice (a summary).* (2014). Retrieved from https://www.cfainstitute.org/learning/foundation/research/Documents/islamic_finance_ethics_concepts_practice.pdf

[157] Thajudeen, Kulsanofer Syed. (2012, September). *Branding Takaful: The Issues and Challenges.* INCEIF, The Global University in Islamic Finance. Kuala Lumpur, Malaysia. p.17 Retrieved from https://www.academia.edu/2321516/Branding_Takaful_The_Issues_and_Challenges

[158] Hohmann Leo. (2105, July 23). *Major U.S.city poised to implement Islamic law* Retrieved from http://www.wnd.com/2015/07/major-u-s-city-poised-to-implement-islamic-law/#QO4QxrGme5OXFrKu.99

[159] Bostom, Andrew. (2008). *The Legacy of Jihad.* Prometheus Books, New York.

[160] Maududi, Sayyid. (1992) *The Economic Problems of Man and its Islamic Solution.* Pakistan. 10th edition. p.42 Retrieved from http://www.muslim-library.com/dl/books/English_The_Economic_Problems_of_Man_and_Its_Islamic_Solution.pdf

[161] *Major U.S. City Poised To Implement Islamic Law.* (2016, January 9). Retrieved from http://www.jewsnews.co.il/2016/01/09/major-u-s-city-poised-to-implement-islamic-law-2.html

[162] Maududi, Sayyid. (1992) *The Economic Problems of Man and its Islamic Solution.* Pakistan. 10th edition. p.43 Retrieved from http://www.muslim-

library.com/dl/books/English_The_Economic_Problems_of_M
an_and_Its_Islamic_Solution.pdf

[163] Maududi, Sayyid. (1992) *The Economic Problems of Man
and its Islamic Solution.* Pakistan. 10th edition. p.44 Retrieved
from http://www.muslim-
library.com/dl/books/English_The_Economic_Problems_of_M
an_and_Its_Islamic_Solution.pdf

[164] ibid.

[165] Hanley, Delinda.(2001, January).*In the Wake of 9-11
President Bush and Muslim Leaders Work to Protect Muslim
Americans.* p. 22. Retrieved from http://www.wrmea.org/2001-
november/in-the-wake-of-9-11-president-bush-and-muslim-
leaders-work-to-protect-muslim-americans.html

[166] Adam, Clymer. (1985, July 14)). *In Short: Nonfiction.*
Retrieved from http://www.nytimes.com/1985/07/14/books/in-
short-nonfiction-111845.html

[167] A summarized definition of author.

[168] Timmerman, Kenneth. (2011, October 21). *Obama
Administration Pulls References to Islam from Terror Training
Materials, Official Says.* Retrieved from
http://dailycaller.com/2011/10/21/obama-administration-pulls-
references-to-islam-from-terror-training-materials-official-
says/

[169] Al-Marayati, Salam. (2011, October 19). *The Wrong Way to
Fight Terrorism.* Retrieved from
http://articles.latimes.com/2011/oct/19/opinion/la-oe-
almarayati-fbi-20111019

[170] ibid.

[171] Reilly, Ryan. (2011, October 19). *DOJ: Holder 'Firmly Committed' To Eliminating Anti-Muslim Training.* Retrieved from http://talkingpointsmemo.com/muckraker/doj-official-holder-firmly-committed-to-eliminating-anti-muslim-training

[172] Islamic Terror on American Soil. https://www.thereligionofpeace.com/attacks/american-attacks.aspx

[173] Hate crime data collection guidelines, p. 24, http://www.fbi.gov/about-us/cjis/ucr/hate-crime/hcguidelinesdc99.pdf accessed February 28, 2011.

[174] 18 U.S.C. § 2331 defines "international terrorism" and "domestic terrorism" for purposes of Chapter 113B of the U.S. Code, entitled "Terrorism." Retrieved from https://www.fbi.gov/investigate/terrorism

[175] Volokh,Eugene. (June 26). *Chief Idaho federal prosecutor warns: "The spread of false information or inflammatory or threatening statements ... may violate federal law. Retrieved from* https://www.washingtonpost.com/news/volokh-conspiracy/wp/2016/06/26/chief-idaho-federal-prosecutor-warns-the-spread-of-false-information-or-inflammatory-or-threatening-statements-may-violate-federal-law/?utm_term=.21b2cc51e44e

[176] Curtis, Michael. (2012, February 23). *Is Sharia Law Compatible with Democracy?* p.2 Retrieved from https://www.gatestoneinstitute.org/2869/sharia-law-democracy

[177] ibid. p.1

[178] ibid. p.1

[179] ibid. p.3

[180] Hohmann, Leo. (2012, September 8). *Obama's '1st Muslim judge' has ties to Saudi regime.* Retrieved from http://www.wnd.com/2016/09/obamas-1st-muslim-judge-has-ties-to-saudi-regime/#3862M4b5B3z7uAlZ.99

[181] Hohmann, Leo. (2016, September 8). *Obama's '1st Muslim judge' has ties to Saudi regime.* Retrieved from http://mobile.wnd.com/2016/09/obamas-1st-muslim-judge-has-ties-to-saudi-regime/

[182] Poole, Patrick, Schmitz, Joseph & Team B II. *Sharia: The Threat to America, And Exercise in Competitive Analysis.* Center for Security Policy Press. October 2010 p. 2

[183] ibid. p.2

[184] https://www.thereligionofpeace.com/pages/Qur'an/taqiyya.aspx

[185] https://en.wikipedia.org/wiki/Linda_Sarsour

[186] Poole, Patrick, Schmitz, Joseph & Team B II. (2010, October) *Sharia: The Threat to America: An Exercise in Competitive Analysis. p. 7.* Retrieved from https://www.centerforsecuritypolicy.org/upload/wysiwyg/article%20pdfs/Shariah%20-%20The%20Threat%20to%20America%20(Team%20B%20Report)%20Web%2009292010.pdf

[187] Mohamad, Akram. (1991, May 22). *An Explanatory Memorandum: On the General Strategic Goal for the Group.* Government Exhibit 003-0085/3:04-CR-240-G U.S. v. HLF, et al.United States District Court, Northern District of Texas. http://www.centerforsecuritypolicy.org/2013/05/25/an-

explanatory-memorandum-from-the-archives-of-the-muslim-brotherhood-in-america/

[188] ibid. p. 74

[189] Quote of Taqi ad-Din Ahmed ibn Tamiyya, 13th-century Islamic jurist. (1263-1328). ibid. p. 75

[190] ibid. p.75

[191] ibid. pp. 274-278 and appendix Explanatory Memorandum

[192] Hamas Charter Retrieved from http://www.terrorism-info.org.il/data/pdf/PDF_06_032_2.pdf

[193] Boykin, William, Soyster, Harry, Cooper Henry & 17 more. (2010, September 22). *Sharia: The Threat to America: An Exercise in Competitive Analysis (Report of Team B II)*. Center for Security Policy Press. p. 21. Print.

[194] The List

[195] Center for Security Policy. (n.d.). *Mapping the Muslim Brotherhood in America, a short course, part 16*. Retrieved from http://shariahthethreat.org/a-short-course-1-what-is-shariah/a-short-course-16-mapping-the-muslim-brotherhood-in-america/

[196] http://www.un.org/webcast/pdfs/SRES2334-2016.pdf

[197] http://www.jpost.com/Middle-East/Abbas-I-do-not-want-to-run-again-for-Palestinian-Authority-president-451689

[198] http://www.aljazeera.com/news/2017/10/hamas-hands-gaza-border-crossings-pa-171031190038739.html

199 http://nypost.com/2017/04/30/mahmoud-abbas-harbors-terrorists-and-still-gets-a-white-house-welcome/

200 http://elderofziyon.blogspot.com/2015/07/dictator-abbas-grooming-saeb-erekat-to.html

201 Pavlich, Katie. (2016, September 9). *Funding Terrorism: US reportedly gave 33 billion to Iran, in cash and gold.* http://townhall.com/tipsheet/katiepavlich/2016/09/09/holy-crap-we-gave-30-billion-to-iranin-cash-n2216061

202 BBC News. (2003, June 9). *Who are Islamic Jihad?* Retrieved from http://news.bbc.co.uk/1/hi/world/middle_east/1658443.stm

203 Australian National Security. (2014, July 11). *Palestinian Islamic Jihad.* Retrieved from https://www.nationalsecurity.gov.au/Listedterroristorganisations/Pages/PalestinianIslamicJihad.aspx

204 Ben Gedalyahu, Tzvi. (2011, November 7). *Iran Backs Islamic Jihad's 8,000-Man Army in Gaza.* Retrieved from http://www.israelnationalnews.com/News/News.aspx/149498#.TrhgmnF4Vow

205 Bedeiin, David. (2005, August 10). *Do US Pressures Determine Israeli Policy?* Retrieved from http://israelbehindthenews.com/do-us-pressures-determine-israeli-policy/4615/

206 https://en.wikipedia.org/wiki/Transjordan_(region)

207 https://en.wikipedia.org/wiki/List_of_United_Nations_resolutions_concerning_Israel

[208]http://www.israelnationalnews.com/News/News.aspx/23896
0

[209]https://en.wikipedia.org/wiki/Israeli_Declaration_of_Independence

[210] Zechariah 2:12

[211] Isaiah 62:7

[212] Psalm 137:5-6

[213] Psalm 147:2

[214] http://vision2030.gov.sa/en/node/149

[215] An IPO is an *initial public offering*, the very first sale of stock issued by a company to the public. To read more: https://www.investopedia.com/university/ipo/ipo.asp

[216] Ezekiel 38:13

[217] Hallinan, Conn. (2016, February1). *Adding Up The Cost of Hillary Clinton's Wars.* Retrieved from http://fpif.org/adding-costs-hillary-clintons-wars/

[218] Schweizer, Peter. (2016, May 1). *One Year of Silence On Hillary Clinton Wars.* Retrieved from http://www.breitbart.com/hillary-clinton/2016/05/01/one-year-silence-hillary-clinton-uranium-deal/

[219] Wehner, Peter. (2015, April). *Hillary Clinton's Bribery Scandal.* Retrieved from http://www.realclearpolitics.com/2015/04/26/hillary_clinton039s_bribery_scandal_355733.html

[220] Becker, Jo, McIntire, Mike. (2015, April 23). *Cash Flowed To the Clinton Foundation Amid Russian Uranium Deal.* Retrieved from http://www.nytimes.com/2015/04/24/us/cash-flowed-to-clinton-foundation-as-russians-pressed-for-control-of-uranium-company.html?_r=0

[221] Mandavia, Megha. (2016, October 21). *Rosatom opens regional centre in Mumbai.* Retrieved from www.nytimes.com/by/mike-mcintirehttp://economictimes.indiatimes.com/industry/energy/power/rosatom-opens-regional-centre-in-mumbai/articleshow/54977000.cms

[222] Mandavia, Megha. (2016, October 21). *Rosatom opens regional centre in Mumbai.* Retrieved fromhttp://economictimes.indiatimes.com/industry/energy/power/rosatom-opens-regional-centre-in-mumbai/articleshow/54977000.cms

[223] Breitbart News. (2016, August 23). AP: Many Donors to Clinton Foundation Met with Hillary at State. Retrieved from http://www.breitbart.com/2016-presidential-race/2016/08/23/ap-many-donors-clinton-foundation-met-hillary-state/

[224] http://www.publicationcoach.com/potemkin/

[225] https://www.nytimes.com/2017/01/23/us/politics/tpp-trump-trade-nafta.html

[226] Zaidi, Deena.(2016, July 8). *The Trans-Pacific Partnership: A Deal That Sanders, Clinton, and Trump All Oppose.* Retrieved fromhttp://www.truth-out.org/news/item/36752-the-trans-pacific-partnership-a-deal-that-sanders-clinton-and-trump-all-oppose

[227] Zaidi, Deena.(2016, July 8). *The Trans-Pacific Partnership: A Deal That Sanders, Clinton, and Trump All Oppose.* Retrieved from http://www.truth-out.org/news/item/36752-the-trans-pacific-partnership-a-deal-that-sanders-clinton-and-trump-all-oppose

[228] Zaidi, Deena.(2016, July 8). *The Trans-Pacific Partnership: A Deal That Sanders, Clinton, and Trump All Oppose.* Retrieved from http://www.truth-out.org/news/item/36752-the-trans-pacific-partnership-a-deal-that-sanders-clinton-and-trump-all-oppose

[229] http://www.thehindu.com/news/international/south-china-sea-and-the-nine-dash-line-what-you-need-to-know/article14485046.ece1

[230]Lake, Eli. (2016, September 7). *Obama's Pivot To Asia Fails to Deter China.* Retrieved from https://www.bloomberg.com/view/articles/2016-09-07/obama-s-pivot-to-asia-fails-to-deter-china

[231] http://www.nydailynews.com/news/world/president-trump-granted-rare-dinner-china-forbidden-city-article-1.3618735

[232] Lake, Eli. (2016, September 7). *Obama's Pivot To Asia Fails to Deter China.* Retrieved from https://www.bloomberg.com/view/articles/2016-09-07/obama-s-pivot-to-asia-fails-to-deter-china

[233] https://www.bloomberg.com/view/articles/2016-09-07/obama-s-pivot-to-asia-fails-to-deter-china

[234] Plitsas, Alex. (2016, October 26). *Fact Check: Pence Was Right About Hillary Clinton's Failure In Iraq.* Retrieved from

http://ijr.com/opinion/2016/10/260666-fact-check-pence-right-clintons-failure-renegotiate-iraq-forces-agreement/

[235] Chambers, Francesca. (2014, November 28). *America ditches decade-long plan to train a full-scale Iraqi army in favor of creating a small force actually able to fight ISIS – instead of running away from the militants.* http://www.dailymail.co.uk/news/article-2853345/U-S-train-elite-force-Iraqis-fight-ISIS-instead-rebuilding-entire-army-again.html

[236] https://www.rt.com/op-edge/363539-civil-war-gaddafi-libya/

[237] Putz, Catherine, Tiezzi, Shannon. (2016, April 14). *Did Hillary Clinton's Pivot To Asia Work?*http://fivethirtyeight.com/features/did-hillary-clintons-pivot-to-asia-work/

[238] ibid.

Write me at *networkingthewhy@gmail.com*

Check out my website and courses:

www.networkingthewhy.co

Follow me on . . .

Facebook:

https://www.facebook.com/kimhadassahjohnson

Coffee with Kim:
https://www.facebook.com/groups/1796187750597095/

Twitter:

https://twitter.com/kimjohnson2on2

Instagram:

https://www.instagram.com/moveyourlifeforward/

Make sure to write a review on Amazon and register at
www.unravelingthewashingtonweb.com

To receive your free gifts as a *Thank You* for reading my
book!

*"Your past becomes your stepping stone for the future.
The most important thing for you to do is, step."*

౮౦

www.ingramcontent.com/pod-product-compliance
Lightning Source LLC
Chambersburg PA
CBHW030423290526
45786CB00001B/104